Sophie Swett

Captain Polly

Sophie Swett

Captain Polly

ISBN/EAN: 9783337076603

Printed in Europe, USA, Canada, Australia, Japan

Cover: Foto ©ninafisch / pixelio.de

More available books at **www.hansebooks.com**

Captain Polly. [See p. 23.]

BY
SOPHIE SWETT

𝔈llustrated

NEW YORK
HARPER & BROTHERS, FRANKLIN SQUARE
1889

HARPER'S YOUNG PEOPLE SERIES.

Illustrated. 16mo, Cloth, $1 00 per volume.

THE ADVENTURES OF JIMMY BROWN. Edited by W. L. ALDEN.
THE CRUISE OF THE CANOE CLUB. By W. L. ALDEN.
THE CRUISE OF THE "GHOST." By W. L. ALDEN.
THE MORAL PIRATES. By W. L. ALDEN.
A NEW ROBINSON CRUSOE. By W. L. ALDEN.
TOBY TYLER; OR, TEN WEEKS WITH A CIRCUS. By JAMES OTIS.
MR. STUBBS'S BROTHER. A Sequel to "Toby Tyler." By JAMES OTIS.
TIM AND TIP; OR, THE ADVENTURES OF A BOY AND A DOG. By JAMES OTIS.
LEFT BEHIND; OR, TEN DAYS A NEWSBOY. By JAMES OTIS.
RAISING THE "PEARL." By JAMES OTIS.
SILENT PETE; OR, THE STOWAWAYS. By JAMES OTIS.
THE COLONEL'S MONEY. By LUCY C. LILLIE.
MILDRED'S BARGAIN, AND OTHER STORIES. By LUCY C. LILLIE.
NAN. By LUCY C. LILLIE.
MUSIC AND MUSICIANS. By LUCY C. LILLIE.
ROLF HOUSE. By LUCY C. LILLIE.
JO'S OPPORTUNITY. By LUCY C. LILLIE.
THE HOUSEHOLD OF GLEN HOLLY. By LUCY C. LILLIE.
THE FOUR MACNICOLS. By WILLIAM BLACK.
THE LOST CITY; OR, THE BOY EXPLORERS IN CENTRAL ASIA. By DAVID KER.
INTO UNKNOWN SEAS; OR, THE CRUISE OF TWO SAILOR-BOYS. By DAVID KER.
THE TALKING LEAVES. An Indian Story. By W. O. STODDARD.
TWO ARROWS. A Story of Red and White. By W. O. STODDARD.
WHO WAS PAUL GRAYSON? By JOHN HABBERTON, Author of "Helen's Babies."
PRINCE LAZYBONES, AND OTHER STORIES. By Mrs. W. J. HAYS.
THE ICE QUEEN. By ERNEST INGERSOLL.
STRANGE STORIES FROM HISTORY. By GEORGE CARY EGGLESTON.
WAKULLA: A Story of Adventure in Florida. By KIRK MUNROE.
THE FLAMINGO FEATHER. By KIRK MUNROE.
DERRICK STERLING. By KIRK MUNROE.
CHRYSTAL, JACK, & CO., AND DELTA BIXBY. Two Stories. By KIRK MUNROE.
UNCLE PETER'S TRUST; OR, FOLLOWING THE DRUMS. By GEORGE B. PERRY.
CAPTAIN POLLY. By SOPHIE SWETT.

PUBLISHED BY HARPER & BROTHERS, NEW YORK.

☞ *Any of the above works will be sent by mail, postage prepaid, to any part of the United States or Canada on receipt of the price.*

Copyright, 1889, by HARPER & BROTHERS.

ILLUSTRATIONS.

CAPTAIN POLLY	*Frontispiece.*	
THE CANDY-MAKING.	*Facing page*	26
POLLY'S INDECISION.	"	42
"'WHY, WHAT!—SYD, CAN THAT BE CAINY AND BOSE ON THE WHARF?'". . . .	"	78
"'IT'S ONLY AN OLD WRECK,' SAID HARRY DAMER, AFTER OBSERVING THE 'EXTRAORDINARY CRAFT' THROUGH THE GLASS"	"	94
"SHE SAW ROY LEANING OUT OF AN UPPER WINDOW"	"	124
"FROM SOMEWHERE APPEARED POLLY, IN A FLASH, BREATHLESS".	"	152
"HE STOOD AWAITING HER, WITH HIS HANDS IN HIS TROUSERS POCKETS"	"	156

Illustrations.

"DEL, IN A VERY STRIKING TENNIS COSTUME,
    WAS SEATED UPON THE RAILING OF THE
    PIAZZA" . . . . *Facing page* 168
DEL AND H. JEANNE WALSINGHAM HIGGINS .   "   184
"THE YOUNG LORD HAD SET HIS HEART UPON
    THE DONKEY CART" . . . .   "   202
"'RELICS,' CRIED JEANNE. 'IF THERE'S ANY-
    THING WE DON'T WANT IT'S RELICS'" .   "   220
"'OH, GET AWAY,' GROWLED SYD. 'I'M SICK
    OF GIRLS'" . . . .   "   244
"DEL DREW THE LETTER FROM HER DESK TO
    READ FOR ABOUT THE TENTH TIME" .   "   286
"AND OH, WHAT AN APPETITE HE HAD!" .   "   302

CAPTAIN POLLY.

CHAPTER I.

"It's frett'n' the hairt out iv him for the ould counthry he is, and oursilves mourn'n' that iver we brought him over. Sure he says praties hasn't the same taste at all, and even the quirks in the little pigs' tails isn't so entic'n'."

They all—Roy and Syd and Polly and Bess—looked with intense pity at the old Irishman who sat on the doorstep in the sunshine, with his head drooping upon his breast. Mrs. O'Connor, who was Nora Henessy, their nurse, before she married "the widdy Mike O'Connor," followed them to the gate.

"It's consumpted he is, we're think'n'," she whispered, "but the docthor says lave him breathe the air iv ould Ireland ag'in, and he's a new crathur. And the brother over there is afther writ'n' for him, and would niver begrudge him the bit and the sup, but anny iv us hasn't the passage-money, bein' that misforchinit wid los'n' the foine pig, and the rint com'n' on, and Denny's croup, and the shmall little grane boogs in the praties."

Carrots, the donkey, started up. Carrots had views of his own, and never would wait for the whole of Nora's grievances, which were always poured out at the gate. Fortunately they were all in the cart, which did not always happen when Carrots saw fit to go. Bess and Syd each with a rein—a compromise effected after a slight misunderstanding as to whose turn it was to drive—Roy standing, and Polly dangling out behind.

"It's orfle to be homesick," said Roy, with vivid recollection of the time when he was first sent away to school. "It takes down the stoutest feller. And when he's old and ill, like that, you know—"

Roy was deeply sympathetic; the line that cut his forehead came out in bold relief.

"I can't give anything," said Syd, in quick alarm. (Roy was always getting up subscriptions, but he headed them himself with all that he could spare, and often more.) "I'm the savingest feller that ever was, but I can't get round from one quarter to another. I owe Bilkins for his rowboat, and Prosser for ice-cream and snapping bonbons—catch me to go to a picnic with girls again!—and I haven't paid for those red lights or my boat-flag, and I have to row with the meanest pair of oars, only fit for girls; any other feller would have had a new pair long ago, and it does seem as if 'twas always when a feller's hardest up you come round—"

"We might have a fair," interrupted Bess.

"Father said the last one was demoralizing,

when you didn't give back change and went around coaxing strangers to buy, and the Lawton girls wanted to manage, and the Brewsters were angry because they were not asked to take a table, and people gambled for the things," said Roy.

(Roy's morals were of the wholly uncompromising kind.)

"It was disgraceful," said Polly; "and worse refreshments I never ate. Old Mr. Mulberry had a stroke of apoplexy, and they had to get the caramels at the bake-shop; and the bake-shop caramels taste like kerosene. I told them how to make them right, but they don't improve."

"There isn't a shop at Green Harbor where one can buy candy that is fit to eat," said Syd, gloomily.

"But we can make such nice candy ourselves," said Bess. "And now Aunt Katharine has sent us those recipes that she has tried, what can't we make? And Diantha says we may have the kitchen all to-morrow forenoon."

Patsy O'Connor and his troubles were slipping out of their minds—all but Roy's; the line in his forehead was still deep.

"There's a great market for good candy in this town, especially while the summer visitors are here," he said. "And if this family has a genius for anything, it is for making candy. I wonder if we couldn't earn some money by it."

"Make candy to sell?" cried Bess.

"Enough money to send Patsy O'Connor home," said Roy.

"Oh, Roy, do you think we could? And what fun it would be!" Bess dropped her rein and stood up in her enthusiasm, although the cart was going, bumpity-bump, down Pigeon Hill. "You and I could buy the sugar and things with the money that we were going to put into the bank for Christmas; but where could we make the candy, and where could we sell it? Diantha is cross about the kitchen, and we do make things sticky."

"There is the old summer kitchen that is never used now; we might hire a cooking-stove and have it set up there," said Roy. (Some planning had evidently been going on behind Roy's deep wrinkle.) "Father and mother told Kate to let us do anything reasonable to have a good time while they were gone, and I'm sure Kate will think anything is reasonable that will do good to the poor. I don't know where we should sell the candy."

"Polly might take it in a basket along the beach at bathing and driving times," said Syd, who was inclined to be a wet blanket.

"I really believe Polly would; but oh, what would Del say?" said Bess.

Del was their almost sixteen-year-old sister, who had returned from a fashionable school in Boston with bewilderingly elevated social ambitions, and a constant terror of being disgraced by "the children." You wouldn't have believed that only a year ago Del would dig clams and ride Rory, the old calico horse, barebacked!

Kate, who was eighteen, and had been at the same fashionable school, was as different as possible from Del. She never seemed to be thinking of what people would say; she made all the family desserts, and dusted the parlors with a pretty blue cap on, and she had a knack with her needle: few rents were so hopeless but that Kate could darn them so they would scarcely show; and if any one had a trouble, from the toothache to the heartache, Kate was the one to go to for consolation. But she didn't like quarrels or differences of opinion; she thought every one ought to give in. That was the only unsatisfactory thing about Kate.

"Of course that wouldn't do," said Roy, seriously. Roy was very serious-minded; it was considered a family necessity to cry "joke, joke!" when anything of the kind was attempted in his presence.

"There's the *High-Flyer*," suggested Polly; "she's in a good location."

The *High-Flyer* was an old yacht that had gone ashore on Darning-Needle Ledge, and been tossed up on to the beach at Birch Point.

"She's all going to pieces, isn't she?" said Bess.

"She has gone all she is going to, and that isn't so very badly," said Roy. "Captain McAllister said she wasn't worth repairing, because she was so old. I believe Polly's idea isn't bad. We could patch the old yacht up a little—the captain would let us do anything we liked with her—and turn her around stern foremost—the cabin is all tight—and build some steps to go up, and put up a gay awning to look pretty. Nobody drives or walks or bathes without passing that yacht."

"It's the very thing," said Polly, with decision. I shall ask forty cents a pound for my nut caramels, and fifty for walnut cream. Drive round through the village, Syd; I want to buy a nut-cracker."

Carrots seemed to realize that something was in the wind. He refrained from backing into old Granny Straw's cabbage-patch, and from making hostile demonstrations against the town pump, as was his custom; he even forsook his deliberate amble, and went kicking and cavorting along, making as much fuss as a small but frantic steam-engine, until he stopped before the principal grocery of Green Harbor with a suddenness which spilled Polly out. (Polly, however, according to the testimony of the others, could not be thrown out so but that she would alight upon her feet.) Bess wished to make an immediate contract for a large amount of confectioner's sugar, but Roy thought they had better wait to hear what Kate would say, but he did stop at Wing the carpenter's, to ask him about the expense of certain repairs to the *High-Flyer*.

If Wing asked too much, he meant to make them himself with the aid of Simeon Grow and Cainy Green. Simeon Grow was a general factotum; the old-fashioned Green Harbor people called him Dr. Damer's "hired man." He took care of the garden, and kept the lawn so smooth that no audacious clover ever dared to raise its head; he drove the family carriage, and sometimes the doctor's buggy, and he knew almost as much about the doctor's patients as he did himself; and he also acted in the capacity of humble better-half to Diantha, the queen of the kitchen. He was a class-leader and sometimes a preacher in the little Methodist chapel. He could cut hair and paint signs and make a miniature man-of-war that would almost cause a boy to run away to sea; and, altogether, he was a man much respected, especially by the youthful population of Green Harbor.

Cainy Green—named Cain by a mother who had more respect for than knowledge of Biblical personages—was a poorhouse waif who acted as "chore-boy" at Dr. Damer's, his usefulness consisting chiefly of "bein' round under foot," according to Quintilla, the "second girl;" but as Cainy was preternaturally tall and lean, as nimble as an eel, and never known to be in the house when he could find any pretext for remaining out-of-doors, this remark was generally understood to be figurative.

Kate was watering her sweet peas when Carrots cavorted up the driveway; the broad trellis upon which they were trained was a mass of delicate color, and the sunset's gold was falling upon Kate's hair, which always had glints of gold in it. She had a fresh, fair complexion, too small a chin, although there was a pretty dimple in it, and her hair was parted smoothly away from her forehead; and the girls generally said she hadn't a particle of style, although some people would as soon have wished the Sistine Madonna to be stylish.

"Oh, Kate—whoa, Carrots, *good* Carrots, whoa!—you'd never guess what we're going to do if Diantha doesn't make a fuss; you'll tell her not to, won't you? Oh, that donkey! I'm one *solid* bruise!" Bess picked her plump person up off the gravel, with a groan. Polly had alighted on the grass, and sat there calmly.

Bess had dropped her one rein, and Carrots, naturally inclined to devious courses, had not lost this opportunity to describe a swift circle, to the sudden lightening of his load. It was Roy who drove him off to the stable in peace and sobriety.

"Oh, Kate!" It was Del, this time, coming across the lawn with an open letter in her hand, breathless with excitement. "Harry is coming home in a yacht, with two or three of his classmates. It's the *Pirate*, Bert Langley's yacht, and they're going to Mount Desert and Campobello and everywhere, and they're coming here on the way; and, oh, Kate, there's

a lord among them—Lord Brentford, a real
live English lord—the same one that Ruth
Grafton met at the dancing-class; she couldn't
get over it! He's not quite seventeen, and
he's a lord!"

"How singular! I always supposed lords
were born grown-up," said Syd; a remark
which Del treated with silent contempt.

"Harry says, oh, Kate! that they will stay
here for a few days, perhaps a week, if there's
anything going on."

"We'll try to have something; we'll make
them have a good time if we can. It's fortunate that Aunt Katherine is coming," said
Kate.

"But the lord, Kate! He'll think we're
aborigines. Can't we make Simeon Grow into
a butler? It is just like Cainy Green to have
grown so tall that we can't put him into buttons! *Some* people in Maine do live like—
like other people. Oh dear, if we were only
poor I could be a heroine like a girl in a story!

I could, Kate, and you needn't smile, and as for that child's sneers—" a gesture of lofty scorn completed the sentence, and Syd, who was the child, rolled over upon the grass as if wholly overcome. "Yes, I could struggle and work like—like a bear, if it were poverty, but to be so common does crush me! And those dreadful children *will* let everything out. But Quintilla *shall* wear a cap, and Bess *must* be suppressed."

"If the fellows can agree upon a captain in time we'll give the *Pirate* an escort up the bay," said Roy, who had come back from the stable and heard the news from Bess, who was not deeply affected by Del's troubles.

"The idea that those silly little cat-boats can't go off on a trip without a captain!" said Del, scornfully.

"We're a squadron, if you please, ma'am," said Roy, good-naturedly, and we may go down to Castine, or up to Portland, before we get back. And the Quoddys think their commodore ought to be captain because they're the oldest fellows, and the Norombegas think their president ought to be captain because they have the most sail-boats, and we think our president ought to be because we have the fastest boats. Let's go and stir the fellows up, Syd, so we can get off in time to give the *Pirate* an escort." And off the boys ran, heedless of the supper-bell, which just then rang out its summons.

"And dinner at one o'clock!" murmured Del, as if a new horror had suddenly struck her. "Oh, Kate—"

But Kate had gone into the house with a suspicion of a frown upon her fair forehead. Kate disliked jar and fret, and always avoided it when she could.

"Ten pounds of chocolate creams at fifty cents a pound." Polly was still lying upon the grass, making very bad figures with a very stubby pencil, but they "came out" to her satisfaction. "Patsy O'Connor can go home!"

she exclaimed, triumphantly. And there was no one at hand to remind Polly of the old story of the milkmaid and her eggs, or of the far-reaching consequences that sometimes follow upon the simplest undertakings.

CHAPTER II.

THERE was high carnival in the summer kitchen where the candy-making was going on. Polly, in an apron of Diantha's, which, although several "reefs" had been taken in it, as the boys said, was still so large as occasionally to impede her locomotion, was the mistress of the revels. She mixed and stirred and tasted, with a deep wrinkle of responsibility, like Roy's, between her brows, and severely rapped the knuckles of all pilferers with her big iron spoon; but when the peppermint mixture dropped upon the buttered paper in perfect rounds, and proved strong enough but not too strong, when the caramels were shown to possess the true caramellian consistency and a toothsomeness beyond compare, and when the chocolate cream drops were declared to surpass any that the confectioner's art had ever produced, then Polly waved her iron spoon triumphantly over her head, and wildly joined in "the Ojibwa," a dance "composed," as Bess said, in the family.

"Oh, them young ones!" groaned Diantha, as the hilarious sounds penetrated to her peaceful kitchen. "What I was a-thinkin' of when I told their blessed ma I thought I could stan' it is more'n I know now. 'You'll have your hands full, Diantha,' says she, and she looked so kind of worried, and along with her paleness and sickness and the doctor sayin' goin' to furrin parts would fetch her up and nothin' else wouldn't, what else could I say but jest that I'd try to stan' it with 'em? But if I'm so nigh distracted when she and the doctor ain't been gone but three weeks, what shall I do before the year's up? My sister, Mirandy, says to me, 'Them young ones

The Candy-making.

will set the house afire before their pa and ma comes home.' "The *house!*" says I; 'if they don't set the river afire *I'm* beat!' Miss Kate she's jest as sweet and pretty as can be, and never no airs nor no temper, but you might jest as reasonable expect a six-weeks goslin' to drive a steam-engine as to expect her to manage them children. And their Aunt Katherine that's comin'— Well, if she don't find more'n *her* match I miss my guess! She'll be terrible shocked at 'em, but she won't know nothin' what to do about it. Real bad children they ain't, neither. Sometimes I declare it seems as if Roy was most a saint; but he's a terrible headstrong one, and if there's anything he don't know he hain't heard of it yet! Bess—well if it wa'n't for havin' her finger in everybody's pie, and bein' sure to tell everything that hadn't ought to be told, Bess wouldn't be so tryin'. Sydney always seems to me to be kind of secretive and underhanded, but whatever he's up to you can be pretty sure he ain't forgettin' to look out for number one! Polly— Well I can't help settin' by that young one though I don't always know what to make of her; she's got a faculty of makin' 'em foller her lead. Their grandpa, when he come up the other day, he put his head in at the kitchen winder and says he, 'Well, Diantha, who's cap'n here?' says he. And says I 'Well, if it ain't Polly I'm beat.' He was terrible tickled, and I heard him callin' her Cap'n Polly. She ain't one neither that seems to want to rule for the sake of doin' it—that would make her a terrible hateful young one —but it seems to come along in the course of nater. Now Miss Del, she wa'n't half so troublesome as any one of 'em when she was little; dress her up and put a sash on her and 'twas all she wanted; but now she's got so high-flyin' in her notions that nothin' in Green Harbor ain't good enough for her. There she comes now, coaxin' and argufyin' with Simeon, that would turn himself into a clown or a jumpin'-jack to please any of 'em, to get him to be some kind of a man waiter that fashionable folks has. No, Miss Del, I ain't goin' to say nothin' ag'in' it; if Simeon's a mind to squeeze himself into that old swaller-tailed coat of your grandpa's that ain't a shadder to him, and make himself look like a corp or a minister with a white choker, why he's got a right to; but when it comes to askin' me, a free-born American, with ancestors that fit in the Revolution, and a good head of hair and not yet aged, to wear a cap, I says firmly *no;* and your blessed ma wouldn't never have asked it! If Quintilla has got her mind worked upon by talk of becomin'ness, I hain't no right to interfere. Any friends that Mr. Harry fetches home will get the best I can pervide, whether he's a French Canadian lumberman, sich as he picked up last summer, or the President. I don't know nothin' about English lords, but if they enjoys their victuals, and knows what manners is, I don't see why 'tain't jest as fittin' a place for them as for anybody. *I* hain't no prejudices."

Del turned a deaf ear to Diantha, and devoted herself to coaxing Simeon.

"If 'twas only jest to stand behind Miss Kate's or your Aunt Katherine's chair, Lord bless ye, child, I'd do it till I dropped if 'twould pleasure any of ye; but ye see it's pleased the Lord to make me consid'able stocky, and your grandpa is so slim. It don't appear to me that I could git into them clothes. And as for handlin' dishes, it's well knowed that my fingers is all thumbs. Dianthy, she won't trust me to carry a cup and sarcer. But don't look so disapp'inted, Miss Del. If so be that I *can*—"

"Oh, Kate! where's Kate?" They burst into the kitchen, Roy and Polly and Bess, in a state of great excitement. "We want Kate to make Syd give us the key of the old wing. He's got it and he won't give it to us, and we can't get in at all. He says father meant him to have it—the idea! And we have no other place to cool the candy, for Diantha won't have it in the refrigerator."

"There are four rooms, one for each of us, and you are a very unjust boy," said Polly, with great severity, turning upon Sydney, who walked, with great apparent nonchalance (hands in his pockets) in the wake of the complainants.

"Yes, and Polly's old studio is there, and all her paints, and my old play-house with as much as forty-leven dolls, and Roy's room, and his squirrels and all his white mice would be there, only they're dead, and his stuffed owl, all locked up as if he had any right, and he won't give us the key!" Bess's incoherent complaints came to an end for lack of breath, and Roy took up the strain, although his fire, like Polly's, was poured directly upon the enemy.

"I don't like the way you behave. It looks to me as if you and Bruce Bennett were getting up some mischief in that old wing. I don't like to have you go with Bruce Bennett, any way!"

"Oh, you don't—don't you, indeed? You're a heavy feller!" remarked Sydney, with withering scorn. But his face wore a very guilty flush.

"There's one thing certain!" cried Bess, as if struck by an idea that was sure to bring the enemy to terms. "You can't come on board the *High-Flyer*, not a step, until you give us the key! You have nothing to do with it, for you didn't give a cent. We wouldn't have minded *that*, if you hadn't been so mean about the key. Now you can't come on board."

"Pooh! who wants to have anything to do with such silly girls' play? I have better uses for my money than fixing up a crazy old boat into a candy-shop. And I don't *wish* to join any Pauper Emigration Society."

These remarks were felt to be very cutting,

and they increased the popular indignation against Sydney. The clamor brought Kate to the rescue, and to her the grievance was rehearsed in chorus.

"Oh, dear, why will you quarrel so?" said pretty Kate, her blue eyes misty with trouble. "Sydney, why don't you give them the key if they want it? Or why don't you others let him have it if he is so obstinate? Those old, empty, tumble-down rooms are not worth so much fuss."

"It's a pity to be so grown-up as not to know that those rooms are the very *cream* of the house," said Polly, who when she was excited was apt to lose her hold upon her r's. "What should we do for menageries or circuses or rainy-day howls if it were not for that wing?"

"Well, well, just let him have his own way for a while and before a rainy day comes he'll give you the key."

There was no redress; there was no real

authority to fall back upon. Oh, if Aunt Katherine had only come when she was expected.

As Syd sauntered away Roy sought a private conference with Polly.

"Syd is up to something," he said, with profound conviction. "He's been spending half his time with Bruce Bennett in that wing. He never will let me in. Father forbade his going with Bruce Bennett and that set of boys. If he should get into any real mischief I should feel as if I were to blame."

"You wouldn't be. Let him 'tend to his own behavior!" said Polly, but nevertheless she looked anxious.

"But I'm older than he and—and different. Girls never have any sense of responsibility," said Roy, with his face tied up into a hard knot. "He says he doesn't think he shall go on the yachting trip, and he wouldn't miss it except for some very good reason. I think it is my duty to get into that wing, and see what he is doing there!"

He walked away after Sydney, presumably to try moral suasion once more before resorting to the extreme measure of breaking into that stronghold of mischief, the old wing.

It was a very old building, this old wing, a remnant of the house which had stood there in pre-Revolutionary days. Certain old associations had led Dr. Damer to leave it untouched, but they had not been sufficiently strong to induce him to protect it from the ravages of time and weather, and the children, who had long ago marked it for their own, found in it freedom from the restrictions imposed by furniture and curtains, company manners, and the general impediments of civilization. Certain servants, notably Nora O'Connor, the nurse, had endeavored to make the wing unpopular by a report that it was haunted (influenced either by the demoralizing effect upon the children of so much liberty as they enjoyed there or by the necessity for a periodical cleaning), but with no greater result than that all the young Damers, being of an investigating and not a timid turn, begged with tears to be allowed to sit up there and see the ghost. It was disappointing to find that Nora O'Connor's ghost was a white lilac bush which could be seen through the house from one window to another, and that the "blood-curdlin' scrachin' and scramin'" she had heard was only the noise that the wind made in an old-fashioned ventilating arrangement in the chimney.

But the old wing was good enough, even without a ghost, and, greatest charm of all, it was their own. Polly and Bess had not very long before succeeded to the rooms owned by Kate and Del, and the sense of novelty and pride of possession were not yet exhausted. It was certainly a high-handed outrage that Sydney had committed. As it was summer and unusually sunshiny weather, he had been having the wing all to himself, but that was no reason that he should think he could lock it up!

Polly had effected a compromise with Diantha, by which the candy was now cooling on the top shelf of the pantry, and Bess had been honored by being allowed to drive to the village with Del, who was going to buy stuff to make caps for Quintilla, who had been induced, by skilful flattery, to consent to wear that "badge of servantude," as Diantha called it. Polly, with her candy off her mind, found Sydney's conduct weighing upon it.

"It's a wonder I didn't tell about that awful noise I heard there, like a pistol, the night he and Bruce Bennett were there till eleven o'clock. It's a wonder I didn't, I was so provoked. He was so red when he looked at me; he thought I would. But Roy is so horribly conceited, and preaches so. Oh, I remember, we unlocked the door once when the key was lost, Syd and I, with a key on father's old bunch! Strange I didn't think of it before. Perhaps Syd was thinking of it when he looked at me so queerly. Perhaps he has taken the key, or perhaps father took the bunch with him."

Polly remembered the very drawer in the old desk in her father's office where she and Syd had found that bunch of keys at the time when Syd kept his fox in the old wing, more than a year before, and she found it in the same place now; there was the very key, too, a nickel one, with little scallops at the top.

"I wonder what he has in there! Perhaps it's only another fox, or some rabbits, or he's educating a guinea-pig, like Neal Russell's, or he and Bruce Bennett are making something; there was that putty dog they made once, that could almost wag his tail; they said he *could* have, only the wag hardened too soon, being putty!—I was little then.

Or, perhaps, they're only getting up a secret society."

Polly's heart beat fast, much faster than Nora O'Connor's ghost had ever made it beat, as she put the key into the door of the old wing.

CHAPTER III.

THE key did not seem to turn very easily. And yet it was a perfect fit. The truth is, the small hand that held it wavered.

"He is a very mean boy," said Polly, and she said it aloud, and with emphasis, although there was no one but Bose, the great Newfoundland dog, to hear. Bose wagged his tail, but somewhat lazily, and looked a little bored. Except for the fact that arithmetic could hardly be expected to be Bose's strong point, one might have fancied from his expression that he was trying to reckon up the number of times he had heard that very remark. For the young Damers were, I regret to say, extremely candid in the matter of personal criticism, none being allowed to remain in any uncertainty concerning the opinion of them entertained by the others.

"He has no right to lock it up," said Polly, with still greater emphasis, and Bose wagged his tail even more feebly. It was certainly monotonous, since he had but just listened to these same grievances in the hearing before the proper authority. A dog of any intellect must wonder why she didn't open the door. Bose got up and barked to expedite matters.

"There's no reason why I shouldn't," said Polly.

And Bose barked louder.

"I have a right to go to my own room—" Bose put his paw upon the key—"but then I should have to go right by his room, and if the door were open I should feel sneaking. It's horrible to feel sneaking. And there was the time he didn't tell of me about grandpa's prize Sweetings, and the time he read Grimm to me when I was getting well of the fever— and he hates reading aloud—and the time he lent me the dollar when I'd spent my missionary money and should have been in awful disgrace (if he *did* charge interest), and Roy is so hard on him. I'll keep the key and I'll tell him I *shall* open it if he doesn't let us in; but I won't do it when he doesn't know it—at least I don't think I will. If I should find out that there was really serious mischief going on there—"

Polly turned away from the door, to the great disappointment of Bose, who barked loudly and pawed the door. She took from her pocket a small, thick, dilapidated book, which she called her diary, and which contained, besides a goodly number of leaves, several receptacles for money and small belongings. Into one of these receptacles she dropped the key with a most resolute expression, and went her way with a comfortable sense of being mistress of the situation without being "sneaking."

She put on her hat, called Bose from his

Polly's Indecision.

persistent efforts to get into the old wing—
a persistency which confirmed her suspicion
that Sydney had nothing worse than a squirrel or a fox concealed there—and went across
the lawn, through the orchard, and thence
over a slope of meadow land which, in spring,
boasted a fascinating brook (into which all
the little Damers had successively tumbled as
a way of signalizing their exit from infancy),
but whose course was now marked only by a
procession of blue flags which looked as if
they were leading a march to the sea. Polly
had some red-and-white bunting over her
shoulder, which had previously served some
patriotic purposes, with which her counter, a
pine board, was to be artistically draped. Beyond the meadow was a little strip of marsh,
in which one was obliged to hop from hillock
to hillock to avoid the mud, a feat which long
practice enabled Polly to perform with astonishing agility, and then there was the beach.
Not very much of a beach, and with more

rocks and pebbles than sand; but if one reckoned the amount of fun that had been and was to be had there! Around the point, towards the river, it widened for a space before it was lost in the wharves and ship-yards and mills which caused Green Harbor to be known as a thriving place; beyond these, farther up the river, Mother Nature got her own way again, and kept her pretty Penobscot lined with gently sloping green banks, or picturesquely rugged and rocky ones.

The *High-Flyer*, out near the Point, had already put on a holiday appearance. She had been raised from the sand a little, and an attempt had been made to right her, although she still presented a somewhat tipsy appearance; a new patch showed here and there on her ancient timbers, and a gay awning fluttered in the breeze above her deck. A throng of deeply entertained boys had gathered around her, and it was evident that she was an object of interest to the summer visitors, who congregated upon the beach at this time of day. Del and Bess, in the phaeton, had stopped a little way off, and Del was gazing doubtfully as if she were not at all sure that it was proper, but still felt that it was not so objectionable a diversion as "those children" *might* take it into their heads to indulge in. Roy and Syd were there, too. Roy accompanied by his wrinkle, and Syd looking sullen. "He's had a talking to," said Polly to herself. But it turned out that Roy's wrinkle had been developed from another cause than Syd's misconduct this time.

"Roy's afraid a high tide would float her off, now she's been hauled out of the sand," called Bess, as Polly approached. "Think of all that lovely candy being carried out to sea! I don't believe it will; do you? It's just like Roy."

"I don't think there's any danger," said Wing, the carpenter. "'Twould take a higher tide than we often have, this time of year, to reach her. But you might get a stout rope and tie her to that big rock, if you was afraid."

Polly thought he was quizzing; every one knew that Roy was inclined to be over-cautious; but Roy immediately went in search of the rope.

"There, I believe that job is done," said Wing, gathering up his tools, and preparing to go home to his dinner. "I wouldn't warrant her for a long voyage, but I guess she's fit for the candy trade!"

Cainy Green was standing near the centre of a group of rough-looking boys. There were strikes both in the shipyard and in the mills, and idleness was breeding disorder, especially among the younger members of the working community. It had been apparent for some time that Cainy was developing a taste for bad company; only the most earnest promises of future good behavior had prevented Dr. Damer from dismissing him before he went away. It looked now as if Cainy had forgotten his promises and was taking advantage of the general freedom from restraint. But Polly, who was in haste to put the finishing touches to the *High-Flyer*, so that they might open shop that afternoon, and was about to send Cainy to the house for a broom and a long-sleeved apron, was startled to see Syd join the group of boys and engage in a low-toned and evidently familiar and confidential conversation with them.

"If he is remonstrating with Cainy Green it won't do any good," she said to Bess. But that was only to hide her fear; she knew very well that Syd was not remonstrating with Cainy Green.

"There are so many bad boys about I'm afraid they'll steal the candy or make a disturbance," said Bess, who had more of an eye for practical than moral difficulties.

"We have Bose to watch," said Polly; "and Cainy," she added, rather faintly. "I don't think he would let any harm come to us that he could help."

Cainy came somewhat reluctantly in answer to Polly's call; the conversation was evidently very engrossing. Syd, when he saw that his sisters were observing him, walked away from the boys, but with a careless air, and with his hands in his pockets. Polly drew a long sigh as she watched Syd's retreating figure.

"It's a very *responsible* world," she said, rather to herself than to Bess.

"You'll get to be just like Roy if you think of things in that way," remarked Bess, sagely. "You have to take things as they come in this world. If they steal the candy, why then we shall have to make more; that's all."

And Polly didn't explain that it was not the candy that she was thinking of.

The "opening" was a great success. Kate and Del helped them to decorate the *High-Flyer* with flowers as well as bunting; old Captain Thatcher, a friend of their grandfather's, who was in the West India trade, sent a basket of oranges and lemons and bananas, and Diantha went so far in atoning for her crossness (Diantha was subject to softening moods) as to make some ice-cream, although she still "didn't think no such public kerryins-on would be approved by their mother, if they *was* for charity."

And as sensations as well as good candy were lacking in Green Harbor, even a small one was welcomed by the summer visitors, and the boat candy-shop drew a crowd, and received a liberal patronage. The first day's proceeds were so large that Bess had to count them over five times to be sure that she hadn't made a mistake (arithmetic it must be acknowledged was not Bess's strong point), and Polly declared that if the weather remained fair for three or four days they should not only be able to send Patsy O'Connor home, but buy him a cabin and a pig when he reached there. (They had discovered by the way of conversation that in Patsy O'Connor's view human felicity was incomplete without a pig.)

There were three fair days, and although the crowds naturally fell away as curiosity was appeased, yet a steady custom remained, and desirable donations flowed in from numerous friends. On the third night the stock was so large that it was found impracticable to remove it to the house as had been previously done, and Cainy and Bose were left on board the boat to guard it. Polly felt some misgivings —they would have been greater if it had not been for Bose—but the others did not seem to feel them, and she half-reproached herself. If Cainy did sometimes stray into bad company, he always seemed faithful to and fond of them.

A heavy shower came on just after they went to bed, and Polly said she was glad of it, if it would only be pleasant in the morning, since it would serve to keep Cainy's associates away from the boat. It would do no harm, since the stock was well protected, and Cainy and Bose could find shelter in the cabin. And so she went peacefully to sleep. She was awakened in the night by the noise of the rain still dashing against the windows. Bess also aroused herself and related a remarkable dream which she had just had, in which the young lord who was coming home with their brother figured, bearing an astonishing likeness to Cainy Green, even to the shock of tow-colored hair standing upright upon his head, and the tendency to outgrow his clothes, which so annoyed Diantha; and he explained that his mission was to buy gum-drops for Queen Victoria.

Polly had only time to remark, sleepily, that she was afraid it wasn't a very polite dream, when Morpheus carried her off again. Something awoke her again so suddenly that she sprang up in bed; the distant barking of a dog, and then a howling noise as if the dog were in great pain. She went to the window;

it was not raining, but one of the thick fogs had come that often dropped down upon Green Harbor like a thick curtain, shutting out all the universe that was more than a yard beyond one's nose. It must be very early in the morning, for the fog was of dingiest slate color (daylight would change it to silver). Again the cry of pain came; it was Bose's voice.

Polly dressed herself quickly. Roy was not at home, but was spending the night with the captain of the yachting squadron, which was to have sailed very early that morning. Sydney was suffering from a sore throat, to which he was subject, and it would not be prudent for him to go out. And, after all, there might not be much the matter. Polly, in her waterproof, slipped softly down-stairs and out of the house. The sound had ceased by this time, and as she could not see across the lawn, she went back for her compass and her foghorn; in that fog it was quite possible to lose one's way between the lawn and the shore, and a little way out of the usual course meant getting deeply into the marsh.

She heard Diantha, a fabulously early riser, already bustling about in the kitchen, and she felt an impulse to tell her where she was going, or to ask Simeon to go in her stead, but Simeon was rheumatic, and Diantha would be very likely to scold and say that it was a "wild-goose chase" to go down there just because Bose had howled, and that she should be "all tried to pieces with them children if their Aunt Katherine didn't come soon." So Polly ran along without saying anything to Diantha—to wish, before long, with all her heart that she had.

CHAPTER IV.

POLLY ran as far as there were landmarks to guide her through the thick fog, but in the meadow, where she could not see the fence, she stopped to look at her compass. I must acknowledge that Polly always felt a little satisfaction in looking at her compass, since Roy had said he "believed there *was* one girl who knew where she was if she couldn't see the sun rise." The compass was not really necessary, since she could hear the sea, which was making much more of a commotion than it usually did in a fog, and it did not prevent her from going so far astray as to get into the wettest part of the marsh, so that it took her a long time to get out, or what seemed a long time, for Polly had now grown very anxious about what might have happened on board the *High-Flyer*, since she had blown her fog-horn several times without receiving any answer, notwithstanding the fact that Cainy was a light sleeper, and the accomplishment upon which he prided himself most, and never lost an opportunity of exercising, was his skill in "tooting" like a horn.

She reached the beach at length, and the stern of the *High-Flyer* loomed through the fog. She went into the water to reach it, but she scarcely observed that.

The deck was a very disorderly place, with muddy footprints all over it, a broken bottle, and half-eaten oranges and lemons scattered about.

As Polly looked about her in astonishment and dismay, a folded paper lying at her feet caught her eye. She picked it up and opened it, handling it gingerly because of its grimy condition. It seemed to contain the vows of a secret society; they were expressed in very high-flown language, and they threatened desperate deeds; but what chiefly struck Polly was the fact that among the names signed to this singular document—names of boys who lived on "the patch," a very disreputable locality—were those of Bruce Bennett and Sydney Damer!

Polly read it over three times, and she never forgot a word of it. She felt bewildered; she did not at all understand what it meant, except that Sydney was in very bad company, in much worse mischief than he had ever been suspected of.

Oh, how could Syd behave so? What should she do about it? Why did their father and mother ever go away? She called Cainy, but there was no answer. She whistled for Bose in vain. She opened the cabin door, and a pair of feet in very muddy boots met her gaze; they were much higher than their owner's head, which was lost to sight in a basket, the cover of which it had apparently broken through.

"Cainy, Cainy, are you asleep? What *is* the matter?" cried Polly, bending over the basket. And then she became aware of an odor which made her recoil in disgust. "Oh, how howwible, Cainy Green! You have been dwinking!" cried Polly, losing all hold upon her r's in her excitement.

But her righteous indignation was lost upon Cainy, who remained soundly asleep.

Polly seized the basket with Cainy's head in it, and shook it with all her strength. This vigorous measure was at length successful. Cainy, with great apparent difficulty, aroused himself sufficiently to withdraw his head from the basket. He fixed a vacant gaze, which gradually became permeated with alarm, upon Polly's face.

"You needn't try to pretend. I know just what is the matter," said Polly, with great severity. And then she weakened a little; the tears came into her eyes. "Oh, Cainy, how could you? when we trusted you," she said.

"I didn't mean to do it, Miss Polly," said Cainy, dejectedly. "I never done it before; but them fellers coaxed me and laughed at me. And we was signin' an agreement and they said it had to be swore to that way, and—"

"Cainy, tell me the truth, was my brother Syd here last night?"

"No, he wa'n't," said Cainy, unhesitatingly; and Polly felt as if a great weight had been lifted off her. "But he b'longs," added Cainy, somewhat defiantly. "He's a revolutionist."

"A *what?*" demanded Polly. She had thought that she was prepared to hear almost anything of Syd, but this *was* astonishing.

"A revolutionist," repeated Cainy, somewhat sullenly; "I don't s'pose you know what that is, and girls can't understand. But we're goin' to make things difrunt; everybody's goin' to be rich. Syd and Bruce Bennett, they ain't like some stuck-up fellers that don't care anything about poor fellers. But I guess I hadn't ought to 'a' told. I don't know what

I was thinkin' of to tell;" a look of alarm overspread Cainy's face; "but it's the fellers' fault for makin' me drink. You ain't a-goin' to tell, are you? Seems as if this old boat kep' a-rockin' and strainin', or is it only my head?"

"I don't know," said Polly, absently. She was thinking about the Revolutionists. The word suggested riot and bloodshed to her mind, but it was only ridiculous for those boys to call themselves so. Perhaps Syd really did feel for the poor, and was trying to help these boys; although Polly was forced to acknowledge to herself that a missionary spirit was not just what one would have expected to find in Syd, and in the family circle he was not distinguished for generosity.

"Are you goin' to tell?" asked Cainy again, with an odd mixture of shame and defiance in his manner. "What's that in your hand?" he added, in sudden alarm, catching sight of the paper which Polly still held. "Where'd you get that? What you goin' to do with it?"

Cainy was so terrified that his shock of tow-colored hair actually seemed to stand more upright than ever, and his small gray eyes, which were so crossed that they habitually looked at his nose, appeared to dilate and to look as straight as any one's.

"I don't know what I may do with it," said Polly, with impressive dignity. "At present I shall keep it."

"You don't know what you're a-doin'," said Cainy, solemnly. "You noticed that reddish kind of writin' that the names was wrote in, didn't you? Well, every feller's was wrote with his blood!"

Polly's face turned pale, and the paper dropped from her hand. Cainy swooped upon it with great agility, and thrust it deep into his pocket, while a faint grin relieved the anxiety and dejection of his countenance.

"You told me a wrong story on purpose to make me drop it! I'm afraid you're a very bad boy, Cainy Green!" said Polly, severely.

"It wasn't a story; it was true; and 'twas Bruce Bennett that wanted it done; we never heard of such a thing; he said it made it more solemn and bindin'. I don't know what they would 'a' done to me if I had lost that paper. I must 'a' dropped it when I was so excited about their takin'—"

"Taking what? Oh, Bose! Bose! how could anything have made me forget him? Have they taken Bose? Cainy Green, have you let those terrible boys carry Bose away?"

"Well, I didn't let 'em. I would 'a' stopped 'em if I could," said Cainy.

"He wouldn't have let them do it; he would have torn them all to pieces unless you told him to go with them!" cried Polly, excitedly.

"Well, I didn't tell him to go with them," said Cainy, doggedly.

"They must have hurt him! I heard him cry! What did they do to him? Where have they taken him?" exclaimed Polly, wildly.

"They didn't hurt him—or they wouldn't,

if he'd 'a' kept still. They put a muzzle on him, and he didn't like it; and they had to drag him to make him go."

"And you helped to put the muzzle on, or they couldn't have done it! Bose wouldn't have let them! Oh, Cainy Green! Tell me this moment what they have done with dear old Bose!"

"They hain't hurt him any," said Cainy, doggedly. "I wouldn't 'a' let him go, only when you've signed that paper, you've got to do what the others 'gree to."

"You must be a very strange boy to sign anything that forces you to be cruel and unfaithful, and a slave!" cried Polly, hotly. "You go, this moment, Cainy Green, and bring that dog back! If they make any trouble, tell them that I'll have them arrested. I know their names, every one of them, and I know what there was in that paper. I could repeat every word of it! It was silly enough for boys, but you wouldn't be allowed to use such language." Cainy knotted his forehead into a sullen scowl.

"It ain't safe for folks that don't b'long to know what there is in that paper. You'd better look out if you *are* a girl. And if you get any of us into trouble your own brother 'll be the worst off of any!"

The mention of Syd made Polly's heart sink, but she kept up a brave front to Cainy.

"I'm perfectly astonished at you, Cainy Green! You're not the same boy! I can't think what papa would say. You can't suppose you can make me afraid of a lot of bad and silly boys. And if you don't go and get Bose at once, this very minute—"

"I s'pose you'll promise not to say anything about that paper, nor the fellers bein' here last night, nor—nor nothin'" (this impressive superfluity of negatives Polly perfectly understood as referring to his intoxicated condition), "if I bring him back all right. I don't expect they've shot him yet."

"Shot him? shot Bose? Oh, Cainy, you don't mean it! They wouldn't dare to do that!"

"They ain't fellers that's *afraid* of nothin'," said Cainy, with profound emphasis.

"Oh, Cainy, go quick! don't waste time in talking! Oh, Bose! Bose! What if anything should happen to him. Oh, dear old doggy! Cainy *go!*"

"You hain't promised yet," said Cainy, with sullen decision.

"Stand aside, Cainy Green! I'll go and get some one who will bring Bose back, and arrest you!"

Cainy planted himself against the door.

"I don't like to hurt your feelin's, Miss Polly, honest, I don't; but you see us fellers can't have this told of. A dog's life ain't nothin' besides that. And they'd all be down on me. And, besides, there's Syd."

"Go, go quick, Cainy! If you bring Bose home safe I won't tell."

"Honest and true, black and blue, sure's you live; hold up your right hand, and swear solum."

"I say that I won't tell, and that's enough. Oh, *won't* you hurry?"

Cainy opened the cabin door, somewhat hesitatingly.

"It's rainin' again, great guns," he said.

"No matter! no matter! run, Cainy! You used to pretend to be fond of Bose. Oh, Cainy, save him!"

It was raining heavily, and the water had come up around the *High-Flyer* so that Cainy was obliged to take a flying leap, and then get wet almost up to his knees. She could scarcely have got off, if Cainy had not prevented her. Perhaps it was wrong for her to make that promise; it might be her duty to tell; but what could she do with Bose's life in danger? Why should they wish to shoot Bose? Perhaps to gratify some spite. If Cainy would only hurry a little faster! She fancied she could see Bose's beautiful soft brown eyes looking appealingly up at her, as they did when he broke his leg and had to have it set. She shut the cabin-door, the rain beat in so violently, and, hiding her face in her hands, tried to quiet herself and bear the suspense bravely. How long it was since Cainy went, and how the rain still beat, and the old boat rocked! It must be one of the high tides! In her absorption, Polly had not thought much about the water before. But perhaps Roy's precaution had not been so unnecessary as they thought, after all. She was glad that the boat was fastened to the rock. Even while she thought of it, something seemed to strike the boat with great violence upon the bows. For an instant it almost "stood on its head," as Polly afterwards explained, and she was thrown from her stool to the floor. Then it made a great plunge downward, and Polly thought she was going to be swallowed up in the depths of the earth, or the sea, she was not quite sure which, and then, suddenly, it was swept far out amid the rolling waves. The old yacht that was thought to have made her last trip long ago was once more afloat!

CHAPTER V.

It was what the old sea-captains and fishermen at Green Harbor called "a spell of weather." They had prophesied that when the rain ceased the wind would change and would carry the fog back to "Shaloo" (they meant Bay Chaleur, where all the fogs were supposed to be born), but instead of that the fog came rolling in thicker and thicker, until one might have thought the Green Harbor wharves were the very end of the world, except for the sounds of fog horns that came from out the mist, some near and shrill, others faint and far away.

Syd sat upon a pile of boxes, on the lobster-factory wharf, which extended far out into the water, and kicked his heels meditatively against the wood. The boat-clubs could not go out on their cruise on account of the fog, so he had lost nothing by declining to accompany them. Most of the members of his club were now over in the boat-house, an informal meeting having been called to talk over the prospects. Syd had decided not to go, and yet he did not feel quite satisfied to stay away. They had voted not to admit Bruce Bennett, his most intimate friend, to membership, and he meant to let them know what he thought of their action. They were a lot of prigs, any way, almost as bad as Roy; they thought they had a right to meddle with a feller's affairs, and tell him just what he ought and ought not to do. He would let them know that he should choose his own associates. There were boys in Green Harbor who, if they didn't wear quite as good clothes as the boat-club boys, knew a great deal more of the world, and how to have better times. *They* were not milk-sops. Moreover, it was, as

Bruce Bennett said, a fine thing to side with the poor and oppressed, and help them to get their rights. Bruce talked about Kossuth and William Tell, and Garibaldi and Napoleon Bonaparte, and Lincoln and Grant, and various Socialist leaders all in the same breath, and Sydney, whose strong point was not history, and who had never troubled himself much about political or social agitations, became quite bewildered in mind, but none the less excited in imagination. Life might become the kind of thing that it was in the startlingly illustrated papers which Bruce smuggled from the post-office and shared with Syd. In the thrilling stories which they read there, the "Red Rover of the High Seas," who was only a boy, captured several large men-of-war, almost single handed (but with frightful slaughter), and "Miguel, the One-Armed Cow-Boy of the Plains," after annihilating a whole tribe of Indians, and putting to rout a company of soldiers, left for foreign

Captain Polly. 71

parts with the entire proceeds of a silver mine, and figured magnificently as a Spanish nobleman in the courts of Europe! Of course life in Green Harbor seemed dull after reading those tales, and it was very hard to be an ordinary boy, when one might be a Red Rover of the High Seas or a cow-boy. Of late Bruce Bennett had been especially interested in tyrants and usurpers; he called the mill-owners and the ship-builders by those names, and sympathized very strongly with the strikers. Syd had not quite liked that, at first, because his grandfather was one of the ship-builders, but since he had joined the "L. L. of R. H. R.," which signified "Loyal League of Red-Handed Revolutionists," he had begun to think it was only just. He didn't quite like some things in the vows which he had been obliged to sign before joining the "league." What would Roy or any of the people at home say if they could see them? The girls would be scared to death. But it was pleasant to be looked up to as a leader by the " patch boys," especially when one was somewhat snubbed by the people at home, and always being scolded as if he were a small boy by his brother, who was only two years older than he. What airs Roy did give himself, and those other fellows at the boat-club, too! Still, it was going to be harder than he thought to stay at home from that cruise. If the weather had been fair, so they could have gone that morning, while he was still in the heat of his anger at Bruce's rejection, he could have borne it; now he hadn't decided by any means to go, but he was considering the fact that his staying at home would make no real difference to Bruce. Roy would have told you, with that anxious and cynical look of his, that "when Syd got as far as that—"

What a tooting of horns there was out in the harbor! But those little fishing-boats couldn't take too good care of themselves in such a fog as this. The *Katahdin*, the large steamer, would be due soon, and her great bow would not loom through the fog until she was close upon them.

No trade on the *High-Flyer* to-day. Probably those girls were tired of it by this time, and didn't care, any way. Girls couldn't be expected to stick to anything. They were lying in bed this morning; Bess was always a lazybones, and Kate had insisted that Polly should not be called, because she had been working so hard, and it was such a rare thing for her not to be up hours before breakfast. Syd wondered whether he hadn't better go over to the *High-Flyer* and see whether Cainy had eaten up all the candy, but on second thoughts he decided to get some hooks and a line and fish off the wharf; he would rather like to be near the boat-house when the boys came out, to hear what plans they had made. As he swung himself down from the pile of boxes he heard excited voices behind him. Some old fishermen had been smoking their pipes in the lobster factory door, a few feet away, but he could not see them; they had probably got into a dispute about politics or the strikes, he thought, but the next moment he recognized Roy's voice.

Was it the fog that made Roy's face look so pale? "What are you doing here?" he said, turning upon Syd with the severe manner which of late he always showed in speaking to him. "Don't you know what has happened? You might be of some use. The *High-Flyer* has gone."

"Gone!" echoed Syd, blankly. He had vague visions of an earthquake, of candy pirates, of some desperate doings of the "League," but not a thought of the real truth.

"Carried out to sea!" said Roy, briefly.

"I never thought that tying her to a rock with a piece of twine was going to hold her," remarked Syd, scornfully.

"It was a cable; it would have held the *Great Eastern*, but it was cut—by some of your friends, I suppose," said Roy, trying to control himself, although his voice shook with excitement. "Where Polly is by this time—"

"Polly!" Syd said it incredulously; he thought it probable that Roy was only trying to make him feel as badly as possible, which he always seemed to take pleasure in doing; but when his eyes met Roy's he knew the truth.

"She is missing; we suppose she was carried off in the boat. But Cainy and Bose must have been there too. Bose, brave old fellow, wouldn't let her drown!"

Roy brought out that awful word with difficulty. He looked more kindly at Syd, seeing the misery in his face. "A half-dozen boats have gone out, and grandfather has telegraphed for the *Witch*." The *Water-Witch* was a little steamer which plied between two small ports on the river when the weather was not quite too foul for safety nor quite fair enough for excursion parties, for which it was in great demand. To telegraph for the *Water-Witch*, which was proverbial for being in an unexpected place, did not strike Syd as a promising measure.

"I'm going out myself," he said, with decision. "That old tub would sink long before you could find out whether the *Witch* was catching porgies or had gone up to Bangor looking for a job. I'm glad Wing put so many new timbers on to that old hull, if you didn't think there was any need of it! I can row like sixty, and I'm as likely to run across her as anybody. And here's one of the club boats lying here."

"See here! I wouldn't take that boat if I were you," said Roy, his pale and anxious face flushing deeply.

"Why wouldn't you? I should like to know if I haven't as good a right as anybody—"

"No, you haven't. It wasn't very pleasant for me, and I tried to do the best I could for you. I couldn't forget that you were my brother—"

"That was great of you!" interpolated Syd, his wrathful scorn getting the better of his curiosity to know what was coming—a curiosity with which was mingled a certain shrinking feeling of presentiment.

"They voted to expel you from the club. I don't know why you should be so surprised. I've expected it for a long time. I've warned you that decent boys were not going to associate with one of the "patch" gang. You ought not to complain of being called one of them; you are seen with them often enough, if it *is* usually after dark. I don't see why you should stand there glaring at me; *I'm* not to blame for it. We can't stop to talk about it now, anyway; we sha'n't care what happens if—if we can't find Polly. *I'll* take the boat, and we'll go together. I can't do any good waiting for the telegram; there are plenty to see to that, and I should go crazy!

I think Cainy can be depended upon to do all that can be done to keep the old boat afloat, and Bose can swim like a fish— Why, what!—Syd, *can* that be Cainy and Bose on the wharf?"

They had gone down the flight of stairs to the slip where the club rowboat lay—Syd in sullen silence—and were about to push off in the boat when Roy, happening to glance upward, saw, dividing the fog, a long, ungainly figure, with trousers too short and coat too long, and a hat which seemed prevented from being an entire extinguisher only by a pair of very big ears. This was undoubtedly Cainy. Diantha had thriftily locked up the new every-day suit which Dr. Damer had bought for him just before he went away, considering that he was under a moral obligation to grow to the doctor's old clothes; and the great, shaggy, yellow heap that broke from Cainy's hold and came tumbling down the steps as if wild with joy was certainly Bose.

"'Why, what!—Syd, can that be Cainy and Bose on the wharf?'"

Roy called, but Cainy had shrunk back and disappeared.

"Have they found the *High-Flyer?* or wasn't he on board?" said Syd. But Roy had sprung out of the boat and rushed up the steps. He seized Cainy by his flying coat-tail. Cainy faced him, but looked as if he would be glad to get away, even at the sacrifice of his coat-tail.

"What does this mean?" demanded Roy, breathlessly.

"I never asked 'em to come there. I couldn't help it if they was a mind to. There was more of them than what there was of me," said Cainy, with a sort of dogged defiance; "and I hid all the best of the candy and stuff where they couldn't get it, and there wa'n't any harm done, and I never drank a drop before in my life, and I was only kind of sleepy, and your own brother b'longs, and they never meant to shoot him. I only told her so to scare her; but they wanted to keep him for a reward, and I had an orfle time to get him; and they said she'd tell anyhow, and I might have known you couldn't trust a girl." Cainy's defiance was weakening under Roy's steady gaze, and he brought his words out as if by a great effort and in spasmodic jerks which made them seem even more incoherent than they were.

"What *are* you talking about?" gasped Roy, remembering vaguely that he had heard of people who had lost their reason by being shipwrecked. "Where did you come from?"

"I've been on an errand. Miss Polly, she sent me. And I couldn't get back before because—"

"Where was she when she sent you?" interrupted Roy.

"She came aboard the *High-Flyer* before five o'clock this mornin'; some girls *ain't* always round findin' out what's goin' on." (Cainy added this remark in an aggrieved tone.)

"And you left her there alone! and she has been carried off to sea alone in that boat!"

"Good land of Goshen, she ain't! That old hulk won't hold together no time! She'll be drownded before she gets back!" said Cainy, cheerfully. "I don't know what she came down for. I was jest gettin' everything ship-shape, in case the sun should come out, and I hadn't let no fellers come nigh nor nothin', and Bose was a-settin' up there as large as life—"

"Come along! You can row," said Roy, sharply.

CHAPTER VI.

THE great wave which had knocked the old *High-Flyer* about, and tossed her out to sea as if she were a feather, had taken to itself, as often mysteriously happens, a far greater volume and violence than the other waves around it. When Polly recovered from her benumbing terror sufficiently to realize what had happened, the old boat, although tossing about much more than was agreeable, showed no further inclination to "stand upon its head," but was apparently being carried by the current rapidly out towards the open sea.

"It is not sinking, it is sailing like any other boat," thought Polly. And she felt grateful to Wing, the carpenter, of whom she had heard people complain because he always persisted in putting two nails where one would do just as well. "But of course it cannot last long. There is something cold around my feet that feels like water now!"

She rushed to the cabin door and opened it. The rain had slackened to a feeble drizzle, but the fog was even more impenetrable. For one dizzy moment it seemed to Polly that a whole world of fog and waves was drifting by her while the old boat upon which she stood remained stationary, and it brought the queerest things to her mind: how the moon followed all the way when she, a tiny girl, took her first evening drive home from grandpa's—a wonderful thing to be out in the night, and find out that the moon was so sociable; and of the first time that she played "ring-round-rosy" too long in the meadow, and the brook and the elm-tree changed sides, as if they were in a dance. How long ago everything seemed, even yesterday, and how far away her home! They considered Polly very stout-hearted at home, but she had her little moment of despair. Then she recovered herself and seized the horn that hung at her side, and blew some vigorous blasts. "At least I will keep vessels from running me down," she said to herself. There were responses to her horn, but they came from far up in the harbor, where the vessels had taken shelter.

"If there is nothing outside here to pick me up there will be nothing to run me down," thought Polly, trying stoutly to be a philosopher. "How queerly the bow sticks up out of the water! That is because she isn't ballasted, and the counters and things in the stern are so heavy. I wonder if she would be likely to keep afloat longer if she were righted. I might possibly manage to throw them overboard."

Polly brought all her nautical knowledge, which even Syd had sometimes generously admitted to be not inconsiderable for a girl, to bear upon this point, and decided not to make any effort to lighten the stern. If the *High-Flyer* should run upon Darning Needle Ledge, which was now her greatest fear, the bow might remain high and dry so that she could cling to it until help came.

Darning Needle Ledge was a line of rocks which, at low tide, showed their jagged points from afar, but had crunched many a good ship's bones while the water lay all blue and serene above them. As well as she was able to judge, with the aid of her compass, the *High-Flyer* was being carried directly towards the ledge. There was a bell-buoy there now, to warn ships off the dangerous rocks, but of what use was a warning to a boat that had neither helm nor sail?

But the boat was settling, Polly thought, slowly but surely; every time that she looked it seemed to her that the stern lay lower in the water. She thought that the cabin must be half filled with water by this time. She need not worry about the ledge; the boat might not live to reach it. Once she thought she felt the boat settle, and heard the water rushing in; she thought it was sinking and cried out in terror. The boat seemed to raise itself again, with an effort, like a living thing, but Polly kept on crying and calling for help, in the hope that some one might be near enough to hear. But her voice seemed to be smothered and lost in the fog; not even an echo came back to her.

Although the stern lay so low, the bow still raised itself grotesquely, but with a triumphant air, out of the water, and the flag which Roy had hung there to give a gala air, although limp and draggled, now and then essayed a feeble flutter.

Hark! That was the bell buoy! It had a weird and ghostly sound in the brightest of days; they always sang their gayest songs when they sailed near it. Kate had said that it always seemed to her to be ringing a knell for the poor people who had been wrecked upon the ledge, and whose bones lay whitening below it. Was it ringing so loudly and solemnly because there was to be another victim? The old boat drifted on, her bow high in the air, and her stern low in the water; and would she pass to the right or left of the buoy? One side meant a little hope of life and home once more; the other—Polly shut her eyes and waited. She tried to say a prayer, but no words would come. She could not even remember "Now I lay me," her brain was so confused; she thought, queerly enough, of the time when the bull chased them in the field and Syd tried to pray, and said "When in the course of human events"! Would God think she was very wicked that she could not even remember "Now I lay me"? Foolish Polly, to think that the confusion of your brain would hinder the All-wise Father's care!

The old *High-Flyer* was in rough water now; she rolled about, and her timbers creaked and shivered; she was passing the buoy; the sound of the bell was growing fainter, but in her bewilderment Polly could scarcely tell upon which side it was. When she dared to open her eyes it was just visible through the fog, swaying monotonously, while the bell kept up its doleful chant. But the *High-Flyer* had passed outside of it, and was at a safe distance from the Darning Needles. Polly could find words for a little prayer of thanksgiving then, but she was becoming exhausted with the long anxiety and excitement, and as she lay huddled in a little miserable heap upon the deck, her eyes, which she had strained so long to search the baffling fog, closed, and the foghorn dropped from her hand.

The shrill scream of a steamboat whistle close at her ear, it seemed, aroused her. A huge black shape loomed through the fog close upon her. She had known that the *Katahdin* would come up to the harbor this morning, but she had not thought of this danger of drifting across its track.

"Keep her off! keep her off, can't you? Hard alee!" shouted voices from the steamer. "What's the matter, cap'n? Are you asleep, or drunk?"

Just in time the huge steamer, huge at least beside the little *High-Flyer*, turned sharply, and went screaming off through the fog, leaving a commotion of waves in her wake that made the little boat leap and plunge. Polly had called frantically to them for help, but the wind which brought their voices to her, carried hers away from them. It afterwards transpired that they had finally concluded that the *High-Flyer* was an old wreck that had got afloat in the storm; they had not seen the wreck's passenger, nor taken into account the possibility that it might have one.

Polly felt as if her last hope had gone with the steamer; the loneliness, too, seemed more awful than before. If she had even Bose with her, dear old faithful Bose, whose peril her own had not made her forget. How like a bad dream it all seemed; Cainy's treachery and the finding of Syd's name on the roll of that dreadful "League;" if she only might wake in her safe, snug bed, and find it to be so!

The water was growing deeper in the stern. Baskets and boxes had floated out from under the seats and the counters, and were sailing about. There was a pail there; she wished she had tried to bail it out at first; there was too much of it now; perhaps it would have been useless, even at first. Nothing could be done now; the old *High-Flyer* had made a longer voyage than any one could have believed possible; it must now be nearly at an end. Polly went to the extreme edge of the bow, which was now farther than ever out of water, and waited.

The *Pirate* was a jaunty little yacht. She sat, as her owner, Bert Langley, was proud to remark, like a bird on the water, and if her name were not altogether appropriate, still, with her rakish build, her black paint, and her decorative skull and cross-bones, she looked as piratical as a boat could be expected to look since piracy has gone so entirely out of fashion. And her owner, who was just twenty-one, and had come into possession of a fortune, was as magnificent in his ideas as any story-book pirate of them all, and had fitted up the yacht with as much luxury as so few feet of space could possibly contain.

But, alas! the good-fortune that always waits upon a story-book pirate had not attended this trip. The sailing-master had been taken very ill with the mumps—a disease which the gay young yachtsman and his guests found it so ridiculous for a stout fellow of twenty-seven to be afflicted with, that they bestowed more scoffing than sympathy upon him. But they were obliged to put him ashore at the first opportunity, and they engaged, without sufficient care, another sailor who was recommended to be the "knowingest pilot along shore." But he proved to have a worse distemper than the mumps, which caused him to quarrel with the steward, smash the dishes and furniture, and the ship's compass, and finally to subside into his berth with his knowingness in total eclipse; and the yacht, without a compass in a dense fog, was at the mercy of such nautical skill as its owner and his youthful guests might possess.

"I'm afraid to go at anything but a snail's pace in this confounded fog," growled Bert Langley, sitting down upon a heap of rope, coiled with naval exactness, on the damp deck, where Josh Faulkner and the young English lord were trying to take views of the fog effects, of which they found an ample variety. "'It's the rockiest and deceivingest coast in North Ameriky,' as the old fellow at Camden told us. We've done nothing but run down buoys for the last three miles."

"Stop growling, Bert; it's really going to clear now. A minute ago I saw blue sky enough to make a Dutchman a pair of trousers."

"A minute ago? where is it now?" grumbled Bert. "But it does look like clearing off there to leeward. If we could make Green Harbor I wouldn't complain if the fog lasted a week. A fellow is sure of a good time at Damer's; it's the best house I know to visit at. Free and easy; the doctor scientific, absorbed in his books, and the mother an invalid; can't make much difference that they're abroad; the small fry run at large, and there's a boy or two much too large for his size. But Kate is what I call a regularly nice girl, and as pretty as a May morning; not too professionally pretty, you know, but good and sweet to look at, and knows how to make a fellow feel at ease, and put his best foot foremost. Del's the beauty of the family, and she used to be a jolly little thing, but they say she is getting 'missish' and puts on airs. There's one they call Polly; red hair and big eyes; rakes you fore and aft with them; makes you feel as if she were seeing whether there was any meanness about you. I wonder how Polly will turn out."

The young lord politely expressed the opinion that Harry Damer's family must be everything that was agreeable. He was a slender stripling, looking less than his sixteen years, with a frank and jovial boyishness, and an unmixed astonishment at everything American. His tutor, detained in a Boston hotel by an attack of erysipelas, had seen him depart alone with much trepidation and many charges; but he impressed an observer as having a fund of prudence and reserve behind his boyish good cheer which made him abundantly able to take care of himself.

Harry Damer came up from the lower regions, where he had been showing the cook how to concoct a salad dressing after a famous recipe of Kate's.

"What an extraordinary craft!" exclaimed Lord Brentford, who was looking through a glass in the direction where the fog had par-

"'It's only an old wreck,' said Harry Damer, after observing the 'extraordinary craft' through the glass."

tially cleared. "She carries her nose in the air, and drags her tail in the water, like a disabled goose. See if you can make her out, Damer."

"It's a new Yankee invention; a fellow has patented it," said Josh Faulkner, who was training himself for a wit. "Anybody can sail ships in the water; we Yankees are finding out that the laws of gravitation—"

"It's only an old wreck," said Harry Damer, after observing the "extraordinary craft" carefully through the glass. "She was aground somewhere, probably, and floated off in the storm. There she goes, drifting off into the thick fog again. She's settling; she won't last long."

CHAPTER VII.

"I can't get that queer little craft out of my mind," said Harry Damer, peering through the glass into the thick fog in which she had been lost to sight. "I couldn't make out that there was any one on board of her, but I fancied I saw something white waved like a flag of distress. I wish you would stand over that way, Langley. It won't be much out of our course, and the fog is breaking away again over there. See! there she is again! She looks like an old yacht that was beached just below our grounds, and used by the children for a playhouse. I don't suppose there is any one on her, but if you *will* stand over there, Langley — it gives me an awful feeling to see her pitching and plunging about there, and know that every moment is likely to be her last!"

"Looks as if there were a little heap of something—might be a dog—up there in her bow!" exclaimed Josh Faulkner, who was proverbially long-sighted. "Hark! that horn comes from there! Dogs don't blow horns! There is some one there! and there's no time to lose!"

Bert Langley was already giving the necessary orders to the two sailors who constituted the available crew of the *Pirate*. She swung around, and with the best speed she could make went in pursuit of the queer little craft, which was now and again so shrouded in fog that they held their breaths in suspense, fearing that she had gone down.

They had come near enough now for Harry to feel certain that it was the old *High-Flyer*, although it seemed impossible that she could have floated so long; and as she was for a moment free from fog, with the space of blue sky large enough for a Dutchman's trousers directly above her, he caught sight of a gleam of color up there in the bow that made him say, under his breath, and with a strangling lump in his throat:

"If that doesn't look like dear old Polly's red head!"

After that the delay which the perverse wind caused was unendurable. A boat was lowered, and Harry and Josh Faulkner rowed swiftly towards the wreck.

Polly had been so brave that I am not going to confess how she broke down at sight of Harry, nor how limp was the burden which Harry's strong arms lowered into the row-boat. Harry, with his sophomore honors thick upon him, and bearing also the proud position of stroke-oar of the 'varsity crew, was absolutely obliged to conquer the strangling in his throat, and pretend, in spite of his white face, to take things calmly, as became a man; and Josh Faulkner felt that it was never more clearly his mission to make jokes than now.

Polly shivered as she looked back at the old boat; she watched it until the fog, which was still very thick farther out at sea, had swallowed it up entirely. Would it go drifting on and on through fog and sunshine, through days and nights, until it reached far-off seas and strange foreign lands; or would it be tossed upon some shore where children would think it a treasure, as they had done, and wonder over its bunting-draped counters and its cargo of homemade candy; or would it very soon " give the mermaids an opportunity to set up shop," as Josh Faulkner prophesied.

She was almost herself by the time they reached the *Pirate*, where she was received with great enthusiasm, and every one and everything on board placed at her disposal. The yacht's misfortunes were distinctly seen to have been blessings in disguise, since they threw her in the way of the wreck, and enabled her to rescue Polly. The compass was promptly produced from Polly's pocket, and with its aid and that of a freshening breeze, which Polly was declared to have brought with her as well as the compass, the *Pirate* made such good speed that before it was fairly dark the Green Harbor lights, the dear lights of home, which brought tears to Polly's eyes, twinkled through the lessening mist.

Polly had found the young English lord somewhat disappointing, he being, as she afterwards explained to Bess, "just like any other nice boy." He was very much impressed by her, knitting his brows over her, and remarking that it was "a very extraordinary country." He seemed to regard it as a feature of the country for girls to go drifting about on wrecks, with compasses in their pockets and fog-horns at their sides, and found it a perplexing social problem.

"It isn't quite fair to throw the responsibility of Polly upon the whole country, you know," said Harry, laughing; but he looked somewhat grave and perplexed as he wondered what the young Englishman, or indeed any civilized person, as he said to himself, would think of them all at Birch Point. They ran wild when their father and mother were at home; what must be the state of things now that they were absent? "Bad children they wa'n't;" he could agree with Diantha's oft-repeated opinion, but he was also inclined to agree with Del that they ought to be suppressed. What would Del have said to know that he was half inclined to class her among the children! The nursery and the school-room were the only proper places for children until they were grown and fit for the society of their elders; and the primitive style of living which prevailed at Birch Point, in which they were continually at the front, was a great mistake. It was so short a time that Harry had held these views that he had not strongly set them forth to the proper authorities. He now regretted this very much. Polly was conversing very freely with the young lord; she was now confiding to him their shop-keeping experiences, and now she was telling him that Cainy Green, their "chore-boy," was a "wevolutionist." (No one with a weakness about r's could be expected to have a stout hold upon them after such experiences as Polly's.) He made it evident, to Polly's great glee and open scorn, that he thought she was bestowing a Yankee pronunciation upon *choir-boy*, and she was obliged to explain at great length the functions of a "chore-boy," of which the young Englishman had never heard. This explanation revealed much of the household economy, even to the fact that Diantha made Cainy wear his employer's old clothes (which was coupled with a promise that he should soon see "how funny Cainy looked in papa's old dress coat) and her (Diantha's) long-sleeved apron when he peeled the potatoes."

The young lord seemed to find the peaceful nature of Cainy's avocations queerly incongruous with the fact that he was a revolutionist. But on this point Polly had become suddenly silent; she had remembered her promise, and Syd's connection with the "League," which in the reaction of her spirits had slipped out of her consciousness like a nightmare in the morning.

Her light-heartedness was gone. The home-lights which had beckoned so cheerfully were clouded by dread. But as the *Pirate* drew near the wharf, and Harry called to some one standing on it, a joyful, an unmistakably familiar bark greeted his voice.

"There's Bose. I shouldn't feel as if I had got home if Bose were not the first to greet me," said Harry.

As soon as she set foot on the wharf Polly seized Bose and hugged him and cried over him.

Out of a shadow appeared Cainy, shuffling and shamefaced.

"I'm runnin' to make a bonfire on the Point, as they told me to, if you was found," he said, standing first on one foot and then on the other, like a perturbed hen. "There's an orfle lot of boats out after you, and everybody's most crazy. Your grandfather, he's aboard the *Witch*."

"Hurry, then, and make the fire!" said Harry.

"Yes, and the bells is goin' to be set a ringin'." Cainy started, but turned back to say, with his voice a trifle husky,

"I say, I'm glad you wa'n't drownded, Miss Polly. I kind of thought at first— But I *be* glad, as sure as you're born."

A crowd surrounded Polly. Familiar faces appeared out of the mist, as if by magic, and in the dim and twinkling lamplight they did not draw themselves down, or straighten themselves out, but showed all their smiles and tears; how sorry they had been for her, the townspeople who had known her from babyhood, and how dear they were to her! She might come to think, again, that old Mrs. Pillsbury was stingy, and that Laura French had said she was "a tomboy," and that Mr. Luke Preble had driven them out of his wood-lot, where there were raspberries; but now they were all kind and glad, and Polly had learned, as she might not have done for years but for that awful, lonely voyage on the old wreck, how sweet is the touch of human sympathy. There was even a kindly grin, here and there, on the faces of the "patch" boys, and little Billy O'Brien, to whom Polly had once done a kindness, drew his ragged sleeve across his eyes—or was it a little lower than his eyes, and for a more obvious necessity? Billy's habits, alas! made such an inference possible, but Polly gave him the benefit of the doubt.

There was a great cheering as they drove off, in the somewhat dilapidated old vehicle which waited about the wharf in the hope of a stray passenger.

Cainy, with the zealous assistance which is sure to be offered to such an undertaking, had made a huge bonfire; the fog seemed to be fleeing before it in ghostlike shapes, and the whole Point was light.

The bonfire was the first intimation of Polly's safety which had come to the family in the house, and, wild with eagerness, they came rushing out at the sound of wheels, among them Aunt Katherine, who had arrived by the *Katahdin*, the same steamer which had so nearly crunched the old *High-Flyer* under her wheels.

They all seized upon Polly with such eager joy as to be quite oblivious of her companions. Del came to herself with a great shock when she heard Harry present Lord Brentford to Aunt Katharine. She was quite overcome when she heard Aunt Katherine say, with simple hospitality:

"Show Lord Brentford into the peacock chamber, Harry. Supper will be ready directly."

How countrified, how common, it sounded! How bitterly mortifying it was after she had worked so hard to arrange seven o'clock dinners after he should arrive, and had evolved a hopeful butler from Simeon Grow, with what "labor dire and weary woe" only she herself knew, and had subdued Diantha's independence in some degree, and brought Quintilla to a cap-and-apron frame of mind, to have this scion of the British aristocracy behold them in every-day keeping; in fact, at their worst—for no one would be thinking of anything but Polly. Del loved Polly dearly; she had suffered so while she was lost that all her plans had been quite forgotten, but now that she was safe, *she did* wish that she could have been saved by some other boat than the *Pirate*.

Aunt Katherine was cultivated and bookish—quite too bookish, Del thought—and she had moved in good society both at home and abroad, and had entertained many distinguished people, but she could not—the worst of it was she didn't *wish* to be—fashionable.

"I wrote to Harry to telegraph from Rockland; oh, why didn't he do it?"

Del made this moan in a state of collapse in the great leather arm-chair in the hall. She made it to the empty air, for the young men had gone to their rooms, and the others had carried Polly off to hers.

"Where is she? where is she?" Grandpa came into the parlor where Polly, who had declined to be put to bed, sat before the wood fire. Grandpa's hands trembled as he stretched them out to Polly; he looked like a very old man, as he never had done before. They all knew that to grandpa there was no one quite like Polly.

"How are you, my boy, how are you?" he said, absently, to the young lord.

Grandpa had been a ship-carpenter, and had worked with his hands in his youth. He had made a large fortune, but he had never, as he expressed it, got a good grip on the king's English. Del had spent many moments of late wondering how grandpa would figure in an English novel; he would be spoken of as belonging to the lower classes, she thought; a lord would not be expected to associate with him. She hoped Lord Brentford would know at once that he had been governor of the state. Roy and Syd came in. Roy had a white line around his mouth, and his lips were set.

"I tied the boat, you know, sir," he said to his grandfather, in a high-keyed, nervous voice that was almost a scream. "I tied it with a cable; it *never* could have broken; it was cut. Now I am going to find out who did it; and if there is any one who knows and doesn't tell—"

Syd's face was white against the crimson

sofa upon which he had sat down. But Polly —it was no wonder, they said, since she had been through so much—Polly dropped her head upon her grandfather's knee and quietly fainted.

CHAPTER VIII.

WHERE was the fog the next morning? Not even caught here and there among the hills, in torn and filmy scraps; not lurking in heavy banks far off, where the sea and sky met. The sun that was looking over the Camden hills with a vigilant eye for a stray bit that it might "burn off," as the fishermen said, had set the blue river and the bluer sea to sparkling and the dewy fields to glittering, and tuned up afresh the bird orchestra that had played its overture, faintly, in the dim gray of the morning; but not the faintest film of fog had it found to try its beams upon. And grandpa, under Polly's window, was whistling "Come lasses and lads," the old tune that was his great favorite. Polly thought, when she first awoke, that yesterday was a bad dream; but Bess, who had rubbed open first one eye and then the other, gave her a great hug. "I woke in the night, all in a fright, and had to feel over to be sure that you were there. Oh, Polly, how awful yesterday was, and what should we have done if you never had come back? I remembered how I wouldn't braid your hair, and how I ran away with Carrots when you wanted to drive him to Belrock. I should have given away my new chatelaine watch; I should never have cared for anything again in the world. The lord *is* disappointing," she continued, more briskly. (Bess's mind was not adapted to entertaining sad possibilities for any length of time.) "Of course, when one comes to think of it, one couldn't expect him to be anything but a boy; but it does seem too bad that he should look like Jimmy Battles, in the post-office."

"Jimmy Battles is very good-looking," said Polly.

"Good-looking for Jimmy Battles, but not for a lord," said Bess.

"Lord Brentford doesn't put on so many airs as Jimmy Battles," remarked Polly.

"Oh, no. I think he is a very nice boy. Did you see how well he and Roy got on together last night? Roy liked talking to him so much that he forgot to tie his forehead up into a hard knot, although he was in such a state of mind because the rope was cut that fastened the *High-Flyer*. I don't suppose you noticed; it was just before you fainted. He screamed out that if there was any one who knew and didn't tell, he was going to have dreadful things happen to them. I knew what he meant. Oh, Polly, can you keep a secret? The club boys have agreed not to say much about it, for Roy's sake and ours, but Rowse Wheelock told Kitty and she told me. If grandpa should know it, he'd have him sent away to that awfully strict school he knows of; and then Syd says he would run away to sea, and I know he would. You won't tell, because that would be awful, and because I promised, but they've expelled Syd from the boat-club. It's because he goes with the "patch" boys; he and Bruce Bennett have been seen with a whole gang of them very often. I talked round and asked Syd what made him do it. I didn't let him suspect that I had heard anything, you know. I only asked him why the club boys didn't seem to like him, and why he wasn't going on the cruise. He colored as red as fire, and he said they were a lot of sneaks, and it wasn't any of my business, and that he was a reformer. And that's why he has locked up the old wing. It has something to do with his being a reformer. I suppose we shall have to speak to grandpa about that if he doesn't open it."

"No, we mustn't," said Polly, quickly, because—"

She was going to say "because I have a key to it," but she stopped herself. Dear

Bess! she meant to be as wise as an owl, but her tongue was like a Jack-in-the-box; with the least little jar of the spring out it popped. It was a family saying that if one told Bess a secret before breakfast, it would be known away up river before night.

"We sha'n't care to go in there while the weather is pleasant, and he may give it up," was what Polly did say. She must have a little private conference with Syd, she thought; and yet nothing seemed more hopeless, for at the first suggestion of blame Syd was always filled with a sullen sense of injury. He never "owned up," as all the others did.

But Polly's tender heart had a great ache for him. There was only a year between them in age, and they had faced the world together—the world that had such keen sorrows and joys—when Syd also wore dresses, feeling their ignominy, and was scorned by Roy; he always had been scorned, more or less, by Roy.

He was proud, and he must be intensely mortified by the action of the boat-club; but he must realize that he had no one to blame but himself, although he would never acknowledge it. If those dreadful boys with whom he was associated had cut the *High-Flyer's* rope, exposing her to such danger, Syd must have suffered, and he might be induced to break with them. Polly thought she might even be glad of her frightful experience if it would draw Syd from evil companions, and resolved, hopefully, to make an immediate appeal to Syd's feelings. If she could coax him to withdraw his signature from that dreadful agreement of the " League." There could not be much meaning in the frightful words which were used, or in the desperate deeds which were proposed. But what would grandpa, or Roy, or any one say to know that Syd's name was there; that he was not only one with the strikers — grandpa himself acknowledged that there were two sides to that matter, and explained it to them carefully, although he felt that he was right in holding out against the demands of his men in the shipyard—but one with the lawless, reckless element that was becoming a terror to the town. If Syd persisted in being a reformer after the fashion of the "R. H. R. League," it might become her duty to tell grandpa. But there was her promise! Polly shivered with an awful sense of responsibility as she thought of it. Cainy had no right to extort such a promise from her, she thought; but, nevertheless, Polly's simple, straightforward mind recognized no circumstance under which a promise might be broken. In the code of morals which had developed in the Birch Point nursery, the blackest of sins was to break a promise. Even Syd would not break a promise, although—well, he did sometimes forget that he had made one.

"I think the hardest trouble in the world is to be very fond of a person who isn't—isn't satisfactory," thought Polly. "Diantha says I don't know anything about trouble, because I am young, but that is what I think."

Ah, Polly! you may live to be far older without changing your mind on that point.

But the world was bright this morning, and home was sweet, after her great danger. Grandpa was whistling and whistling, which meant that he wished some of them to come down. Perhaps the things that troubled her would all turn out according to Bess's prophecy about the strikes. "Oh, they'll come to an end soon, disagreeable things always do," was what Bess had said, and Polly resolved to pin her faith to this cheerful creed, if she could. In any case she would not worry and be always scenting danger from afar, like Roy.

So, in a more hopeful mood, Polly carefully adjusted the folds of her new blue cambric dress, and tied a fresh blue ribbon upon her long braid. Del had, of late, been giving them all salutary warnings against carelessness in the matter of dress, which, I am sorry to say, Polly often needed. This morning she was trim and dainty enough even for grandpa's eyes, which Polly thought in her heart were much more important than the English lord's, since he was, after all, only a boy; trim and dainty, and "as fresh as a pink rose in the morning," as grandpa often said; but Del was in the habit of remarking, with a despairing accent, that she didn't think Polly would ever have any "style."

Diantha's voice floated up from the kitchen regions, as Polly went down-stairs.

"Boys is boys, and it ain't for an old woman like me to curchey to 'em. Not that I ever thought of layin' it up ag'in' him that he was a lord, seein' he hadn't no choice about it. He's real kind of boyish and pretty-spoken, and no more airs than nothin' at all. I declare if it wa'n't a real prover-dunce that they come so unawares that Del hadn't time to rig poor Simeon up for a butler! I guess she'd 'a' found out that 'twould take more'n her grandpa's old dress coat and a minister's choker to make Simeon like city folkses' servants. If he's got a weak point, it's table-manners and handlin' crockery. And to think of expectin' a consid'able portly man like poor Simeon to put himself inside of the governor's coat, that hain't no more figger'n' a shad. Land! I dreamp it had busted clearn down the back, and Simeon was tryin' to hang himself atop of the dinin'-room door with the white choker, and I woke up all in a cold presperation."

"My gracious! no wonder," said Quintilla, sympathetically. "But I wish I had only dreamp what that boy Cainy has just been and gone and done! Miss Del said he was to be sent up this morning to take the lord's boots—'his lordship's boots,' that's what Miss Del said, that would be set outside his door, and when he'd cleaned 'em and carried 'em back he was to offer to wait upon him, for it was most likely he'd been used to a valley. That's what Miss Del said. *I* don't see, for the life of me, why folks couldn't wait on themselves just as easy on high land like this; but there ain't any such thing as keepin' track of Miss Del's notions. She told me just what Cainy was to say, and I drilled him in it till I thought I should 'a' dropped. Miss Del promised to give me her pink feather fan if nothin' went wrong that I could help while the lord was here. I didn't expect I could do nothin' with Cainy, because he's awful down on lords, and he said anyway this one was an imposertor, because he didn't have a crown on his head, and an ermine cloak, like one he saw in a jography; but he's an awful ignorant boy, and I told him so, to think anybody but Queen Victory herself would go round yachtin' and fishin' dressed up like that. Anyhow, I got him to do it; he seemed to feel kind of humble and meachin' on account of not takin' better care of the boat and Miss Polly, and he said it all right over and over after me, 'My lord, can the boy do anything more for you?' And I listened after he got up to the door, and if he didn't say right out, as loud and plain as could be, 'My *boy*, can the *lord* do anything more for you?' I thought I should sink right through the floor; but you'd ought to 'a' heard his lordship laugh, right out hearty, just like anybody. And he gave Cainy a quarter, and if that aggravatin' imp didn't come downstairs a whistlin' 'Yankee Doodle,' when I'd warned him pertickerler not to do that for fear of hurtin' his lordship's feelin's. I expect he did mean to say it right, but he got confused. He says he knows he ain't a lord, now he's seen him, because he's just like any feller. He's ringin' the quarter out on the steps, now, to see if it ain't a bad one, because he says folks in the village says the lord is most likely an imposertor."

"There ain't nothin' but ragamuffins that's so imperdent, I'll warrant. Folks that *is* anything knows that our Mr. Harry is used to aristocracy, and would know a lord the minute he clapped his eyes on to him," said Diantha, with somewhat inconsistent pride.

"He seems too young for Mr. Harry. And I think he takes more to the younger ones. At the table last night Master Roy was promisin' to take him where there was Indian mounds and arrow-heads; and la', you'd think they was talkin' about a gold mine, they was so excited; and then Master Roy had him upstairs showin' him his collection. He'll be takin' him up into the old wing to see his snakes and things next."

It was a good thing, thought Polly, as she tripped light-heartedly out-of-doors, that Roy had found a sympathizer in his pursuits; he could not give his whole mind to Syd's misdeeds. It was of no use for Roy to be so hard upon Syd, it only made him worse. She was running through the garden in search of her grandfather, when she heard her name called, in a low and mysterious voice, and, looking in the direction from whence it came, discovered Roy standing in an upper window of the old wing, with his forehead in its hardest of hard knots.

"Come up here! I want to tell you something," he said.

"*She saw Roy leaning out of an upper window.*"

CHAPTER IX.

HAD Syd given up the key of the old wing? If he had it was surely a promise of better things, Polly thought hopefully. For Syd was so very obstinate. His father quoted Hosea Bigelow, "when he's sot, the meetin' house ain't no sotter," and prophesied, lightly, that he would learn better "one of these days;" his mother sighed over him, and his grandfather shook his head; but they all spoke cheerfully of what the future was likely to do for him, and no one took him very seriously except Roy, who was, indeed, inclined to take every one seriously, himself included. And Roy, according to Polly's theory, only "made him worse." Syd never gave up. Could his expulsion from the boat-club have brought him to a better mind, Polly wondered.

Her doubts were solved by the sight of the step-ladder at one of the windows and a broken pane of glass. Roy had evidently broken in. He looked as if he might be in a mood for desperate measures. Polly tiptoed hesitatingly into the dark hall, feeling a vague fear of what might be concealed there. Red-handed Revolutionists might spring out of any of the dark corners. The creaking of the stairs made her heart jump.

"He refused to give me the key, so I was forced to break in," said Roy, standing, very erect and deeply flushed, at the head of the stairs. "It wasn't a pleasant thing to do. I might have decided to appeal to my grandfather"—Roy always used the possessive pronoun to an unusual extent when he was dignified, and it was felt to be very impressive—"if he had not been sent for, from home, on account of a new trouble. I felt that it would be wrong to add to his anxieties. Besides, I don't like his plan of sending Syd to school as a last resort. The discipline might be good for him, but I know what a large school is; there are plenty of nice fellows, of course, but if a fellow is naturally inclined to gravitate towards evil associates—"

"Oh, dear me!" said Polly, and dropped down upon the highest step. Roy's dignity and large words were always wofully disheartening to her; they seemed to enlarge troubles like a microscope. And yesterday's strain had left her weak to bear new troubles.

"What did you want to tell me? What have you found, Roy?" she said, falteringly.

"Come here!" beckoned Roy, walking backward down the corridor to the door of Syd's room.

Painted upon the door was a mysterious device, composed of a red hand clinched in a menacing position, the American flag, a sword and a pistol, and the letters "L. L. R. H. R." There was some difficulty in discovering exactly what the emblems were, but the lack of artistic accuracy was abundantly atoned for by brilliancy of coloring, and the effect was startling. Polly drew a breath of relief. If that was all, she had seen that before.

"It is evidently the badge of a secret society, and I'll tell you what I think it is: a society of the worst roughs in town, and they have their meetings here. When he has pretended to have a sore throat, as an excuse for going to bed at seven o'clock, he has crept out here and held orgies with that set. I have suspected it, and I have tried to catch him, but he is too sly."

"Oh, Roy, it may not be as bad as that!"

"I have seen him sneaking into the house at one o'clock at night, and boys going away from here; one I am almost sure was Nick Hiffley."

Nick Hiffley was a big boy of eighteen, known as a ringleader among the turbulent spirits of "the patch."

"I shouldn't be surprised to know that they

went directly from here to set my grandfather's barn on fire this morning. Yes, it was burned almost to the ground; they only just saved the stock. My grandfather stayed here last night; they probably knew it, and took advantage of it."

"Oh, poor grandpa! they will worry him to death. I wish he would give them all they ask for, and have some peace!"

"Sometimes I think you are rather superior, Polly, but that is just like a girl," said Roy, with lofty scorn.

"I think you are too hard upon Syd, Roy," said Polly, her spirit rousing a little, as it was apt to do under Roy's scorn. "I think you are taking things for granted. A great many boys might be taken for Nick Hiffley in the night; and to say that they may have gone from here to burn grandpa's barn!—it sounds as if you meant that Syd had something to do with it."

Polly's own doubts, and the consciousness

that her defence was even more lame than the accusation was vague and indefinite, made her tones more indignant than they might otherwise have been. The treble armor of "him who has his quarrel just" gives a calmness which Polly could never feel in defending Syd. And yet Syd *could* be accused of greater misdeeds than he had committed.

"I don't know why it is," said Roy, with some irritation, "but unless you're *very* mad about something he has done to you, you always stand up for Syd. I should think after you have almost lost your life as a consequence of his keeping bad company you would feel anxious to have some efforts made to reform him. Do you suppose those fellows would have dared to cut that rope, or to have gone near the *High-Flyer* at all, if Syd hadn't associated with them? No, I *don't* mean that he cut the rope, or knew of it, but he encouraged them to come there. I have reason to think that this precious society"—Roy waved his hand with great oratorical effect towards the startling device upon the door—"held a meeting on board the *High-Flyer* the night before, and that Syd was among them!"

"Oh, no, he wasn't! he wasn't there at all!" cried Polly. "I *know* he wasn't."

"How do you know?" demanded Roy, quickly. "Were any of them there when you went down in the morning? Were there any signs of an orgie? I mean in the *real* meaning of the word."

Poor Roy! he was forced to make this explanation because the word, being a great favorite of his, had begun to be used in derision by the others to designate a very mild form of entertainment. Syd and Polly and Bess indulged in "peanut orgies," and "ice-cream orgies," and Syd even went so far as to call the high-school exhibition an "education orgie." These things Roy suffered with a manifest but dignified sense of injury, and he used the word no less often, but always with an explanation.

But Polly had no need to try to "smother a grin," as Syd would have said, on this occasion. She was too much depressed by her troubles, and the difficulties attending a cross-examination by Roy.

"Things were not in very good order, but there was no one there but Cainy," she said.

"Why did you go down there at that time in the morning? And what sort of an errand did you send Cainy on?" demanded Roy.

"I don't know why you should question me in that way. I may have had reasons," said Polly.

"Oh, if you are keeping the secrets of the 'L. L. R. H. R.—' There Polly! don't get angry. I know well enough that they wouldn't trust those to a girl. But I don't see why the affairs of that candy-shop should be private. I wish it had never been done. I don't see how I ever consented to it."

"It was you who proposed it," said Polly. "Poor Patsy O'Connor! there's enough money to send him home. That's *one* good thing."

"A dear passage!" said Roy. "We had better have saved up all of us. I say, Polly, Syd has been buying curtains. I looked through the keyhole — a fellow doesn't like to do such a thing, but it may be his duty. They are felting, or damask, or something thick, like those. And he has been trying to borrow money of me to pay his honest debts!"

"He has been awfully short," said Polly, not without a sympathetic accent.

"Why is he always short?" demanded Roy, judicially. "Doesn't he have the same allowance as the rest of us, and isn't he always begging of grandpa besides? When a boy gets into bad company—of course he squanders money."

"Curtains are not so very squandering," protested Polly, feebly.

Roy made a gesture of impatience. "I mentioned his being short in connection with those only because it showed how necessary they must have been to induce him to spend money for them. There is something in that room that has to be hidden! The blinds are closed, and the curtains drawn tightly over every possible chink. And listen? do you hear that queer little bubbling noise?"

Polly did hear it, and had a wild, momentary vision of witches' cauldrons, and of the giant who smelled the blood of an Englishman, and declared his intention of grinding his bones to make his bread; for scarcely less murderous were the avowed purposes of the "L. L. R. H. R.'s." But the next moment she was saying, stoutly: "There may be no harm in a queer little bubbling noise. Syd has a right to have queer things in his room if he likes. You had live snakes, once, and we didn't sleep a wink; and I *don't* think it's nice to listen at people's keyholes; and what can you do about it, anyway, if you are not going to speak to grandpa?"

"I was foolish to think that a girl could understand a moral responsibility," said Roy, with gloomy scorn. "Of course I must speak to my grandfather as a last resort. But first I shall talk to Syd, seriously."

"Oh, let me, Roy!" cried Polly, winking away some stray tears from her lashes. "You have done it so much, and, indeed, Roy, I don't mean to say anything unkind, but you do have a *superior* way that makes him angry. I've been meaning to try to coax him not to go with those dreadful boys. Do let me, Roy!"

"*Let* you? why, of course, I shall be only too glad to have you. Do you suppose I enjoy nagging at a fellow all the time? Why will you all misunderstand me so? I only want to do what is right and best."

"I know you do, Roy dear, and Syd *is* dreadfully trying. But you have to smooth him just the right way, or you only make the sparks fly. Did you tell him that you wanted the key because you wanted to show your snakes to Lord Brentford?"

"Of course I didn't. I *demanded* the key because I had a right to it."

"I wonder if people don't always have to give up more or less to their own, when it isn't reasonable; and I wonder whether it isn't sometimes wiser to ignore one's rights," said Polly, in a speculative manner.

"It may do for girls to be managing like that. Men never are," said Roy, loftily.

Polly secretly resented the adjective, but put her theories into practice by taking no notice of it.

"Anyway, it wouldn't have made any difference with Syd," said Roy, after a moment's thought.

"I am not sure that it would have," said Polly, candidly, and then she sighed.

"Of course you couldn't give up showing

your collection to Lord Brentford," she said. "Does he like snakes?" Roy's face cleared instantly.

"I never met a fellow whose tastes were so much like mine. He knows more about some things, but not so much about others. It is worth the while to show things to a person who can appreciate them. Of course a fellow doesn't really mind having them called rubbish, but ignorance is always trying. I am very glad that he is going to stay. Haven't you heard? Langley is obliged to go down to Campobello, directly, to meet his mother, and Lord Brentford wants to stay where he could get a telegram from his tutor; the yacht may be a long time on the way, you know. I think he wants to stay, anyway. He accepted Aunt Katherine's invitation very promptly."

"It will be great fun to have him," said Polly, with enthusiasm. She was thinking in her heart that it was what Diantha called a "Providence," that this should happen to take Roy's mind from Syd's misdeeds.

But not even a congenial friend, with an interest in snakes, could make Roy forget his present anxiety.

He bent his head to the door again.

"The noise is a little different, now. It's a kind of puffing and fizzling. It may be steam."

"What can it be?" The question faltered on Polly's lips, as Syd's face, white and angry, appeared above the stair railing.

CHAPTER X.

"It isn't surprising to find *some people* peeping through keyholes," said Syd, with withering emphasis; "but one might have expected better things of you" (to Polly).

She might have denied that she had peeped, but listening was much the same thing, and she felt that it would be cowardly to leave all the ignominy to Roy. And she couldn't rid herself of the feeling that it was ignominious in spite of Roy's elaborate justification of himself in the name of duty.

"We have a right to come in here, you know. And you had no right to force Roy to break in. He wanted to show his collections to Lord Brentford," she said.

"Why couldn't he have said so, then?"

growled Syd. "I wasn't going to give any of you the key just to spy upon me. A fellow has a right to do what he pleases in his own room."

"You leave us in no doubt as to the character of the visitors you receive there," said Roy, pointing a scornful finger at the startling device upon the door.

"They're not fellows that go mooning round, chloroforming bugs and sticking pins through them, and they haven't all swallowed a dictionary, but they have some brains, and they know how to mind their own business. That's an accomplishment that doesn't seem to come easy to some people who think they're very swell. I hope you have made as many discoveries as you expected to through my keyhole!"

"If I had wanted to spy upon you, Syd, I needn't have waited for Roy to break in." And Polly produced her diary, and took the key from it. "I've had that all the time."

"I remembered that key! I looked for it in father's desk," said Syd. "You must have been there before me. Do you mean to say you didn't—"

"I must say I think that was very strange of you," said Roy. "There's the glazier's bill, and all the trouble."

"You didn't tell me you were going to break in to get to your collections," said Polly. "I thought I should feel better to have Syd give us the key. I felt sure that he would."

Syd kicked the walls with his heels, in a discomfited way.

"That feller has been asking for you," he said, somewhat hoarsely, to Roy.

Roy understood that "that feller" meant Lord Brentford, and his face cleared a little. But he lingered, his mind evidently burdened with the duty of "talking to" Syd. Polly gave him an appealing look, and to her surprise he responded to it by walking off in silence. Syd drew a long breath of relief.

"If ever a feller feels grateful it's when Roy makes him a present of his back," he said.

"Syd, who burned grandpa's barn?" said Polly.

"Grandpa's barn? Who? When?" demanded Syd, excitedly. "No, I didn't know it. I've just got up. I'm going out there right off, this minute."

"Syd, did the boys who belong to that—that society have anything to do with it?" Polly pointed to the mysterious letters on the door.

"Who says it's a society?" asked Syd, flushing and looking keenly at her.

"Roy and other people. They say, at least, that you have a great deal to do with the 'patch' gang. Oh, Syd, those dreadful boys, who take advantage of the strike to make disturbances and worry grandpa almost to death!"

"Grandpa doesn't do right," said Syd, stoutly. "He is growing richer all the time, and they are growing poorer."

"Some of the mill-owners may be wrong, but grandpa is'n't," said Polly, with decision.

"If that isn't just like a girl!" said Syd, sneeringly.

"Wasn't he a workman once himself, and doesn't he know how to sympathize with them? And didn't he give them what they asked until they went so far that it was ridiculous? And that's all the fault, he says, of the bad ones, who want to quarrel, and not to work. And the bad ones are those boys that you—"

"Now, Polly, there are some things that a girl doesn't understand, and had better not meddle with. What does a girl care who is poor and hungry, or whether there's any justice in the world, so long as she has all the fol-de-rols she wants? No, I don't know that that is quite fair for *you*, Polly"—a slight compunction seemed suddenly to seize Syd—" you are *pretty* good *sometimes*. But it is very foolish for a girl to meddle with deep things, and —and politics."

Polly laughed. A laugh lay always near the surface with Polly, however sad or serious she might feel. It made some people think that she was very light-minded; but they were not very discerning people.

"Syd, Syd, wait a minute!" she called, for Syd was running down-stairs. He looked back at her with a little impatient scowl. "We used to have such good times before you—you grew so different. I can't bear to have you so, Syd. If you would only promise me to break off with the boys who do those dreadful things!"

"A feller can't always do just as he wants to. Sometimes he gets into things before he knows it, and then— But I sha'n't do any dreadful things, I'll promise you that." He was gone, but he came up the stairs again far enough to look through the railing. "I say, Polly, if you know anything that isn't your business, you had better forget it; that's all!" His face wore an anxious frown that made him look like Roy. "You're not much of a telltale, for a girl, but it's safer not to know some things."

Syd looked really anxious, but there was an unmistakable air of importance about him, nevertheless, which tried Polly's temper. He did not seem to feel in the least degree guilty, and he was warning and advising *her!* that was so like Syd.

"I'm not likely to be afraid of a lot of silly boys who think it smart to pretend to be wickeder than they are!" she cried, hotly. But Syd was out of hearing. A minute or two afterwards she saw him come out of the stable on Carrot's back, and the donkey, being in a cheerful morning mood, went careering off at a great speed. Polly felt like huddling herself into a corner of the deep window-seat in the corridor, and having a good cry; she felt tactless and good-for-nothing and tempery and miserable; and Syd was so provokingly un-get-at-able and uncertain—so like Syd. She seemed to have done no good at all. She wished she had asked him what that queer noise in his room was. She wished she had tried to find out why those boys wished to steal Bose, and whether there was any danger of their doing it again. She wondered if she should always be able to keep Roy from finding out what she knew about that society. She wondered if it were not her duty, in spite of her promise, to tell her grandfather about the agreement. Although she had called them foolish boys to Syd, the desperate words kept repeating themselves over and over in her mind. "To slay, burn, and destroy, and to crush under Freedom's heel everything that stood in the way of Equal Rights and the Sovereignty of Labor." Where could they have found such high-sounding phrases? Bruce Bennett, she thought, must have composed the agreement. Could they have thought

that grandpa's barn stood in the way of Equal
Rights and the Sovereignty of Labor? And
the one who was to do the desperate deeds
was to be chosen by lot, and he was not to
shrink from doing them, even at the peril of
his life. Could it have been they who set the
fire in the cotton-mill, which was discovered
just in time to prevent a great conflagration?
No one had suspected boys; but then no one
had known of that society, with its desperate
resolutions. Polly felt more strongly than
ever that it was "a very responsible world."
I am afraid that if her present thoughts had
been put into words there would have been
scarcely an r among them; but her simple
code of morals offered no exception to the
rule that a promise must be kept.

But Syd had promised her that he would
not do dreadful things; there was some comfort in that; for never since a very small and
toddling person, with a great dread of being
laughed at, she had confided to Syd her first

"secret," that she "*was* afraid of the effelunt at the circus because his tail was his nose and his nose was his upper lip"—never since that first trial of his honor had Syd failed to keep his word to her. And there was no time for a good cry—Polly often failed to have time after she had planned to have one—for the breakfast-bell was ringing, and Polly's woes were not so deep but that she could feel a lively curiosity in the matter of Simeon's appearance as a butler, and a keen desire to discover whether the English lord would prove to be, on longer acquaintance, so comfortably like a very nice American boy as he seemed.

But it appeared that Aunt Katherine's counsels had prevailed, or that Del had decided that Simeon would show too plainly that he was a butler, as Syd said, "for this occasion only," for Simeon, in his own proper habiliments, and whistling with unwonted cheerfulness, was rolling the lawn-mower, and Quintilla waited at table as usual, but in her white cap and apron, which were certainly improvements upon her ordinary calico dress and not always tidy hair. Polly fervently hoped that Lord Brentford really observed them more than he seemed to do; she privately thought it rather stupid of Del to take so much pains, but since she had done so it would be a great pity to have Lord Brentford no wiser than if they had a maid in calico, like the rest of Green Harbor. Bess, on her part, felt that this would be an unendurable misfortune; and Bess's tongue always felt that it had a mission to set things right.

"I suppose our Quintilla's cap and apron make you think of England, don't they, Lord Brentford? Del had to coax and coax to get her to wear them; girls in Green Harbor have such foolish notions; but we're going to try to make her wear them after you're gone, aren't we, Del? I think Simeon would have been a butler if—"

It was Harry who stopped her, with his

foot, under the table, to her surprise and indignation, for she felt that she had shown great tact and discretion in her manner of calling Lord Brentford's attention to their elegance. But Bess was quite accustomed to finding her efforts unappreciated, and did not take it much to heart. Del colored furiously, especially as she heard a half-suppressed giggle from Josh Faulkner, who never had any manners, and a faint flush showed itself even on Aunt Katherine's calm cheek, as she met the perplexed gaze of the young Englishman. She went on talking quite easily with him about his travels, however, and Bess was ignored, while Harry made an inward resolve to write to his mother about that matter of having the youngsters relegated to the nursery when there were visitors. Except for that momentary perplexed glance, it was not apparent that Lord Brentford had heard anything about Quintilla's cap, or the butler that might have been, but that it made an impression on him may perhaps be inferred from some entries in his diary, in which he was recording at some length his views of America.

"Don't like the girls so well as our own girls. They seem to be born grown-up, and always have their back-hair on their minds. They never have a good time for fear they are not fashionable. A thirteen-year-old girl— Polly, by name—in this family is not like that; seems like a Hausmutter, and takes responsibilities. Apparently mistress of the situation, cast away on a wreck with compass and a foghorn; struck me that she would be equally so in command of a Cunarder. Must in justice remark, however, that she is not in the least bold. Shall know better what to make of her when I have been here longer. Strikes in the town, and disturbances which are increasing and cause anxiety. Sullen boy in the kitchen, who wears the cook's apron and assists in culinary duties, is, as Miss Polly has told me, a revolutionist. What with American types, strikes, Indian relics, and beautiful specimens, I find the place very interesting.

"P. S. I have just had a queer little adventure. As I was crossing the orchard towards the shore, where my friend Roy, the naturalist, was waiting for me, a brick came flying over the wall, and fell at my feet. From somewhere appeared Polly, in a flash, breathless.

"'Oh, that was intended for me!' she cried. 'I saw Nick Hiffley (or some such name) skulking behind the fence.'

"But I had already picked it up and read, in black letters, upon it,

BEWAR YOU AR WOTCHED.

"I felt as if I were reading a penny dreadful; but Miss Polly, although excited, was evidently not surprised.

"Some things in this country are worthy of praise, but the girls are very extraordinary."

"From somewhere appeared Polly, in a flash, breathless."

CHAPTER XI.

THE " very extraordinary girl " who was destined to furnish many an item for the English boy's American notes looked for one startled moment at the impressive warning printed upon the brick, and then she hopped lightly over the stone wall, and ran, like a deer, in pursuit of the thrower.

"Good wind and a clean stepper," said the English boy to himself, enthusiastic if inelegant, as he watched her. "I do like a girl who can run. But can she be running after the blackguard who threw that brick? Nick Hiffley, she called him, or some such name. Perhaps, however, she is a revolutionist, too? I think, perhaps, I had better go on. She seems perfectly able to take care of herself, and I shouldn't like to get mixed up with treasons, stratagems, and spoils!"

Polly, for her part, was not thinking of Lord Brentford at all. She didn't even wonder what he thought of her, as Del would have done. She had seen an old hat and a pair of stooping shoulders rise, for an instant, above the wall, and her first impression was that they belonged to Nick Hiffley. The next moment, however, she was seized by a suspicion that it was a more familiar figure than Nick's. It seemed to Polly a perfectly natural and proper proceeding to try to find out. A crouching figure was hurrying along, apparently almost on all fours, close beside the wall; as the sound of footsteps reached its ears it arose to an erect position, and set out upon a rapid run. It was an ungainly, slouching figure, and as it ran a pair of long coat-tails were spread to the breeze.

"Cainy! Cainy Green! Stop this moment!" called Polly. The ungainly figure still ran on, but with backward glances, and some slackening of its speed, until, at length, just as Polly's "wind," which Lord Brentford had commended, was almost spent, it came to a halt. Cainy was evidently deliberating between surrender and a short cut across the wettest part of the marsh, where even the dauntless Polly would come to grief.

"If you *don't* stop, Cainy Green—" cried Polly, her temper increasing as her breath shortened; then she remembered that Cainy was apt to be impervious to threats, and tried a different method.

"I want to ask you a question, Cainy," she called, as calmly as was possible under the circumstances.

And Cainy, either because the marsh was most uncomfortably wet, or because he knew that Polly was persistent and reckoning-day would come, decided upon surrender. He stood awaiting her, in an attitude that was half-defiant and half-guilty, with his hands in his trousers' pockets, and his crossed eyes apparently surveying the tip of his nose with deep interest.

"Yes, I throwed it," said he, desperately forestalling inquiries, as Polly reached him. "I cumposed it, and I wrote it, and I throwed it, and there wa'n't nobody else that had nothing to do with it; and, you may believe it or not, it wa'n't so much because I was afraid of bein' took up myself as I was afraid of other folks's bein' took up! If I come and told you, why, then you wouldn't believe me. I thought you'd think somebody else throwed it, and mebbe you'd be scairt."

"Why shouldn't I have believed you, Cainy?" said Polly, severely, seizing the opportunity for a moral lesson.

"Well, I—I'm common folks, and I've been town's-poor," said Cainy, meditatively digging his heel into a bog-hole. "Folks ain't apt to b'lieve town's-poor."

"You *know* that has nothing to do with it!

"*He stood awaiting her, with his hands in his trousers pockets.*"

If no one believes a boy it is the boy's own fault. It must be *dread*ful not to be believed. It's almost the unmanliest thing in the world to tell lies. Cainy, if you'll promise me solemnly to try never to tell another, I'll promise to begin this very day to believe you! Wouldn't it be comfortable for you to know that somebody did?"

Cainy looked up quickly, swallowing meanwhile a lump in his throat. Then he grinned broadly, but the grin was evidently somewhat forced, and soon faded.

"Folks has threatened to lick me for lyin', and folks has promised to give me suthin if I wouldn't, but nobody never promised to b'lieve me before. I ruther guess I'll agree to that."

"It may be pretty hard at first for both of us," said Polly, frankly, "but I'll do my part."

"You was always better to me than any of the rest of 'em, and I was sorry the other day when you was adrift on the *High-Flyer*. I was, honest; if— I hain't forgot the time that they said I drownded the kitten that fell into the old well, and you was the only one that believed I didn't."

"Oh, poor Spotty!" said Polly, with a pang of recollection. "No, I never believed you were so bad as that."

"Diantha says I'm a limb, and I expect I be, but I never drownded Spotty," declared Cainy, solemnly.

Polly suddenly returned to even heavier troubles than the untimely fate of Spotty.

"Cainy, do you know who burned grandpa's barn?" she said.

A "no" arose to Cainy's lips, but was suppressed, an immediate tribute to the strength of his new agreement.

"A feller might know things that he hadn't no right to tell, and then again he mightn't," said Cainy, strictly non-committal. "Anyhow, the guv'nor means to find out; there's an orfle big reward offered, and he's jest *a-tearin'* round."

"Cainy, when you hinted about some one's being arrested, did you mean— Whom did you mean?"

"When there's such goin's on as there is in this town, it might be one and it might be another," said Cainy, shifting uneasily from one foot to the other.

"Did you mean that Syd had anything to do with it?" said Polly, with an effort.

"He never had nothing to *do* with it," said Cainy. "He never knew 'twas goin' to be did."

Polly drew a long, long breath of relief.

"But the fellers that b'longs has to stick by one another," added Cainy, shaking his head solemnly.

"Syd would never stick by any boys who did such things as that!" cried Polly, in the confidence which had come with her sense of relief.

"Fellers that's took oaths has to stick to 'em, I tell *you*. Girls don't understand such things; the fellers say they don't. They're orfle mad at me about your seein' that paper. They was goin' to turn me out. I guess I ain't smart enough for 'em, anyhow; they only let me b'long 'cause I lived here, and they thought they could find out things by me. There's things they'd darst to say to me that they wouldn't darst to say to Syd."

"Oh, Cainy, if they want to turn you out why don't you let them? They're wicked boys, and you'll get into dreadful trouble if you go with them."

"Well, I thought I didn't care if they did, at first, but I *be* a revolutionist, you know; them's my princerples; and then it ain't safe to know so much about 'em and not b'long to 'em. That's one reason why I give you that warnin'; that and 'count of Syd. Bruce Bennett, he wanted to make a plan to get hold of you and make you take an oath, but Nick Hiffley said he wouldn't have any such foolishness. He's gettin' kind of sick of Bruce Bennett; he says, Nick does, that Bruce thinks it's all foolin'. I guess he didn't know, him and Syd, when they joined that the Revolutionists was in dead earnest. I heard 'em talkin' together, and Bruce, he said he was afraid it wa'n't goin' to be so much like a story as they thought. You see, in a story a feller never comes out at the little end of the horn, but in truly livin' he's orfle apt to, 'specially when he gets with a lot of older fellers that makes him do jest as they say. And I'm one of them kind that always gets found out. Fellers in stories never do. I'll tell you what, Miss Polly, Diantha, she says I'm a limb, and I expect I be; most folks thinks so; but if I didn't b'long to them Revolutionists, why then I wouldn't!"

Polly hailed this avowal with delight, as a sign of improvement in Cainy's morals; but he showed her that he was influenced rather by a fear of consequences than by a love of virtue by immediately adding, with great feeling, "It ain't no joke for a feller to get took up. And when the guvnor gets down on a feller he jest goes for him like a thousand of brick. The Revs, they think they're safe, count of havin' the guvnor's grandson amongst 'em; he wouldn't like to see him shet in jail; and Bruce Bennett, his father's a lawyer; but I can't feel safe nohow, I'm such an orfle unlucky feller. You see them two fellers wouldn't be 'lowed to leave, and I expect they'd think 'twas kind of mean to, even if the goin's on was more'n they bargained for."

"Oh, what a dreadful thing it is for boys to get into bad company!" said Polly, with a despairing accent. "There seems to be no end to the trouble that it makes."

"They ain't no cowards, them two fellers ain't," pursued Cainy, ignoring the moral reflections which experience had taught him were apt to have an embarrassingly personal bearing. "Nick Hiffley told 'em they mustn't be scairt if they found that the Rev's guns was loaded with more'n powder."

"Oh, Cainy, they *don't* have guns?" cried Polly, her face paler than it had been on board the wreck.

"I can't say as they do, and I can't say as they don't," said Cainy, changing rapidly from one leg to the other, "but I'll tell you what, Miss Polly," mysteriously lowering his voice, "there's more things than guns that goes off and kills folks!"

"I think you are only trying to frighten me, Cainy. If things are really so bad as that, of course I *must* go to my grandfather and tell him all I know," said Polly, in great distress.

"I didn't think you was one to break a promise, anyhow, Miss Polly," said Cainy, in quick alarm. "And I only *said* that, true as you live, I did. They never told me they had nothing that would go off, true as I'm sett'n' in this chair." (Cainy had evidently quite forgotten, in his excitement, that he was standing, first on one leg and then on the other, almost over shoe in the marsh.) "All that made me say it was something I overheard Bruce Bennett and Syd talkin' about. They seemed to have something or other that they could blow folks up with, but they didn't say they was a-goin' to. I'm a-tellin' you the livin' truth, now, if you don't believe it."

It was evident that Cainy was so unaccustomed to being believed that he never expected to be under any circumstances.

Roy and the young Englishman were coming up from the beach; they passed at a little distance, talking earnestly together; the latter gave Polly a quick, curious glance, perhaps with his notes on American girls in his mind, but Roy found entomology always a more satisfactory study than the ways of girls, and it struck him as nothing unusual that Polly should be talking to Cainy. He had not yet begun to share the young lord's suspicions that Polly was a revolutionist.

Polly only glanced absently at them.

"I do believe you, Cainy," she said. "But you needn't warn me again. I'm only afraid for Syd—and you. Papa had great hopes of you, Cainy."

Cainy looked shamefaced, and was evidently moved, although he tried to grin recklessly.

"I don't calc'late I'll ever be anything but a limb," he said, with a real sadness in his voice.

"But you will remember that I shall believe every word you say?" said Polly.

Cainy regarded her with serious incredulity.

"I'll try not to get you into no scrapes by it, but I'll tell you what, Miss Polly, when a feller is so used to it as I be, lies kind of tell themselves; they do now, honest."

"It is very easy to tell lies, sometimes; I have to try hard not to."

"You don't, now, honest? You ain't foolin'? Well, I never!" exclaimed Cainy, regarding her with open-mouthed astonishment.

"You didn't suppose you were the only one

who was ever tempted to tell lies, did you, Cainy?"

"Well, no; but I expect I *be* the biggest liar that ever was, don't you, Miss Polly?" asked Cainy, anxiously.

It was an acknowledged fact in Dr. Damer's household, and, indeed, in all Green Harbor, that Cainy was without a rival in this particular, and Polly was somewhat embarrassed for an answer.

"So much the more credit to you, Cainy, if you stop lying altogether," she said. "And, Cainy, do get out of that dreadful society!" And away ran Polly.

Bess came to meet her.

"Oh, Polly!" grandpa has found out who burned his barn. It's a gang of boys; and they burned the mill, he thinks, and there's a warrant out for their arrest. But grandpa acts so queerly about it. He was as white as a sheet; and he looked all of a sudden like an old, old man. I told him so, and I asked him what was the matter, and he said, '*Elizabeth*, go into the house!' and there was the English boy standing by. Grandpa *never* spoke like that to me before. Polly, what do you suppose makes him feel so?"

CHAPTER XII.

POLLY answered Bess irritably, and pushed her aside almost roughly.

"Oh, don't ask me, Bess! How do you suppose I know? Go away, Bess; *do* go away!" And she ran by her in search of her grandfather. She should not dare to ask him any questions, she knew; but if she could see his face she thought she could judge as to how deeply Syd was involved in the trouble. But he had gone away in the direction of the village, Simeon said. Roy and the young lord had also disappeared. Del, in a very striking tennis costume, was seated upon the railing of the piazza, talking, in a somewhat excited tone, to Aunt Katherine and Kate, who were quietly devoting themselves to their embroidery.

"*Del, in a very striking tennis costume, was seated upon the railing of the piazza.*"

Polly looked back to where Bess stood, looking cross and injured, and heaved a sigh.

"I wish I were not so excitable and cross. I dare say grandpa was only worried, in a general way, after all. There doesn't seem to be anything the matter."

Certainly Aunt Katherine looked serene, and so did Kate, but then they almost always did. Del seemed to be troubled; she was gesticulating energetically with her tennis racquet; but Del's troubles were apt to be fashionable ones. Polly, like the boys, held them in utter scorn.

"Roy knew that the Swaseys had asked us to play tennis this morning, and he knew it was almost the only place in town where I cared to take Lord Brentford, and he went and planned that excursion across the bay, after Indian arrow-heads and such rubbish, and *made* that boy say he would rather go there. He has been here four days, and he hasn't been anywhere or done anything that I have planned; he hasn't been *entertained* at all; and none of you seem to realize how absurd it is to treat a lord in this way. And I asked Harry, before he went, to put a little item in the papers, here and there, just to say that we had him, and he put on a horrified air, and said he was ashamed of me."

"And no wonder!" said Polly, heartily.

"No one is talking to you, child," said Del, with cutting carelessness. "What *he* thinks of us—"

"But he is only a boy, Del, and he seems to be enjoying himself in a boy's way," said Kate. "I quite congratulated myself on the good time he was having."

"Good time! well, if steeping his soul in bugs with Roy and romping with the children is a good time!" said Del, with great scorn. "But it isn't as if the question were altogether of *his* good time; if he were properly managed, as Jeanne said, in her last letter, he would have made us well known in society everywhere. We might have gone to Newport and New York and Washington and been received—"

"Oh, Del, do wait until the preserving is done!" laughed Kate.

"That's it! that's just the trouble!" said Del, indignantly. "It's a dreadful thing when the eldest daughter of a family has no social aspirations. One would think we might have some position when grandpa has been governor four or five times. Jeanne says that ought to count for a great deal, and she knows; but we never get our names into the paper, no one in society ever heard of us, and grandpa—well, if all the crowned heads of Europe should visit grandpa, he would ask them to sit down on the back porch and have a mug of cider!"

"Oh, Del Damer!" cried Polly, indignantly. "I think grandpa has *beautiful* manners."

"It might be just what the crowned heads would like best," said Aunt Katherine. "To give of yourself as you really are is the best way to entertain people. It can't be any pleasure to them to see you struggling painfully to ape the fashions to which they are accustomed."

Del reddened indignantly.

"I'm sure I don't try to ape any fashions," she said. "I'm only trying to bring this family up to a little more civilized standard; and I'm sure it's discouraging enough without being hindered by—by any one else."

Aunt Katherine looked kindly at the red and angry face of her niece.

"You have certainly done well in some ways," she said, gently. "Polly and Bess, and even the boys, are much more careful about their dress than they used to be; and I know the credit is largely due to you, because your mother has told me so; and I see various little dainty touches about the house that your ambitious little fingers have made; but oh, Del dear"—Del's little smile of gratification faded as she began to see that there was to be a pill in the jelly—" I wish you would see how wicked, how vulgar this struggle after fashion and display is. There is nothing in it but envyings and heart-burnings and vexation of spirit, and it poisons all the sweet and simple and wholesome pleasures of life. To see girls as young as you given up to it, as one does everywhere nowadays, is enough to make one heart-sick!"

Aunt Kate was not given to such "preachments." Kate looked at her in astonishment, and Del had, for the moment, no answer ready.

"You found no pleasure in going to play a delightful out-of-door game with your friends, this beautiful morning," pursued Aunt Katherine; "you were thoroughly angry and miserable because you could not have the glory of displaying a lord as your guest. It was not that you cared for the society of the boys—"

"Indeed it wasn't!" interrupted Del. "Boys of that age are apt to be simply a nuisance."

"They are as old as you ought to be; and Roy is remarkably well-informed, and I have found the young lord very interesting, because he seems a simple, honest, manly boy, and because of his rank, too, because it has given him surroundings and opportunities of great advantage. They might have injured some young persons, but, thank Heaven! the boys are still more sensible."

"Aunt Katherine," said Polly, solemnly, and with a great sigh, "I don't think you could possibly think boys were sensible if you knew them as well as I do."

"It is simply that you don't understand," said Del, who had recovered herself. "And I might as well try to show colors to a blind man as to make you and Kate understand society. Kate is perfectly contented to live out of the world."

"Dear me! I thought I had hosts of friends," said Kate.

"A very mixed lot," said Del, contemptuously. "And Fanny Hunter, whose grandfather was vice-president and a foreign minister, and who has lived in Paris almost all her life, is just the same to you as Prue Philbrick, who worked in a factory to get through Bates College, and teaches school at the corner now, to take care of her paralytic old shoemaker grandfather. You would be quite as likely"—Del waxed warmer as Kate's numerous perversities appeared before her mental vision—"*quite* as likely to invite Prue to meet very distinguished people as Fanny!"

"More likely, perhaps," said Kate. "I shouldn't be able to resist giving Prue an opportunity to learn something. She's such an eager little soul."

"I suppose you think that's very nice, but it isn't the way of the world, and it isn't sensible, and you'll see what you'll come to!"

This somewhat vague prophecy being received only with half-suppressed smiles by her aunt and sister, Del continued:

"I am thankful that Jeanne Higgins is coming. I shall have somebody to stand by me, and I want Lord Brentford to see that we know *some* stylish people, though I don't feel sure that he knows the difference. He doesn't seem to notice grandpa's grammar in the least. Yesterday grandpa said something horribly bad, and he had occasion to say it just afterwards, and he said it in the same way—not making fun a bit, but perfectly serious. There's a pretty story for you! an English lord talking bad grammar."

"I dare say you might find many a one who did," said Aunt Kate, "but Lord Brentford speaks unusually good English for a boy, and I think it was very delicate and polite for him to do as you say he did."

"I thought afterwards that perhaps he did it on purpose, though I didn't know quite what to make of it. I suppose he does see how many mortifications I have to bear, that none of the rest of you seem to care anything about. Jeanne has trouble like that; her own father is a dreadfully rough, ungrammatical old fellow, but he has made lots of money, and they keep him out of the way."

Aunt Katherine's brows contracted, as if something hurt her, but Del seemed quite unconscious that she had convicted her friend's family of either vulgarity or heartlessness. "I wish you had invited Ruth Grafton, instead," was all that Aunt Katherine said.

"Ruth Grafton! I might have asked her for Polly," said Del, with great scorn. "She's like a little girl, if she is almost sixteen. She never appears when there's company, and she has never had a silk dress or a bit of real jewelry in her life. They're very aristocratic; they're one of the oldest families in Massachusetts, and they can trace their ancestry back to William the Conqueror, and I like to know Ruth, but I must say I've got beyond her. I think a girl who is almost sixteen ought to have some society, if she isn't really out, and she certainly ought to have something to wear. I want you to see the bracelets that Jeanne's aunt sent her from Paris!"

"I used to know her mother in Byfield," said Aunt Katherine. "She was Hannah Jane Walsh."

"Yes, and that's Jeanne's name; that's another of her troubles; but she writes it H. Jeanne Walsingham; of course it is changing Walsh a good deal, but it sounds so much better, and she says she really *has* to, although her grandfather doesn't like to have her, because Higgins sounds a little common, too. You can't blame her for that, Aunt Katherine, for I've heard you say you thought every girl ought to have a pretty name."

"There are better things than prettiness," said Aunt Katherine, who was evidently not disposed to make any allowance for H. Jeanne Walsingham Higgins. "I like to see a girl have some sentiment about the name her parents gave her, especially if it's her mother's name."

"She hasn't really changed it," said Del; "and I think that is very nice of her, for she used to cry because her name wasn't Gwendoline. Jeanne is so sensitive. And she has red hair, almost as red as Polly's, though I don't think it quite so bad a shade."

Polly winced a bit at this sisterly frankness. She didn't like her hair, although grandpa had privately assured her that it was the most beautiful color in the world, and he was glad that one of them had grandma's hair.

"And she has it done so stylishly that it looks—oh, quite differently from Polly's, of course. Her mother's maid does it. I'm sure I don't know how she will get along here; and I know she won't think much of Lord Brentford. She's *quite* beyond him. But she will like to say that she has met him."

Aunt Katherine's brows contracted again, but Del was too much absorbed in her own affairs to observe it.

Polly was regarding Del critically, with her

head on one side, wondering if she could be the same Del who only a year ago had liked the wildest kind of a romp, and cared no more for style than the others did. Polly fervently hoped that she should not be sent to Boston to a fashionable school. Del never seemed to have a bit of a good time now, and she was very ridiculous; she called her (Polly) a child! When one is thirteen and a half, one does not like to be called a child. And when the person who puts on such airs is "shaky" in her multiplication table, and constantly asks help of the "child" in the matter of French verbs and German umlauts, it is especially aggravating. And then about the red hair!

Polly "kept in," but was very red in the face, and she kicked her heels against the steps on which she sat, until Aunt Katherine looked up in surprise at the clatter. And she had almost forgotten about Syd and all the trouble, until Aunt Katherine, who evidently did not care to say all she thought about the aspirations of Del and her prospective guest, suddenly changed the subject by inquiring whether either of them had seen Syd. He had not appeared at breakfast, and his grandfather had been searching for him in vain, and she supposed that he must have gone fishing, although the day was not very favorable.

"Oh, that reminds me," exclaimed Del, "that I woke very early this morning, it couldn't have been four o'clock, for it wasn't fairly light, and I saw Syd and Bruce Bennett going out of the drive-way with a hand-cart such as the rag-men have. It seemed to be full of something, and it was covered with an old sail. They handled it carefully, as if it were something breakable, or very precious. I heard Bruce Bennett say, 'It's orfle risky! It may be the last of us!' They went off towards the village. I didn't think of it when grandpa was asking for him. I wonder if he hasn't been at home since. Don't look so frightened, Aunt Katherine, it's only some of those boys' nonsense. Nothing ever happens to them. There's that old carriage from the landing. If it isn't coming here! It can't be Jeanne! I really believe it is! Oh, why didn't she let me know? What will she think? That's always the way when distinguished people come, while, if it's old Aunt Abigail, from Cherryfield, we get there with a coach and four!" Del rushed down the steps as the clattering, creaking old vehicle turned into the drive-way, while Polly, even with her heart full of anxiety about Syd, as it was, peeped curiously from behind a sheltering pillar of the piazza for the first possible glimpse of H. Jeanne Walsingham Higgins, with the stylish red hair.

CHAPTER XIII.

There was only a glimpse to be had of a stylish travelling-dress, and a dainty veil and ribbons, as Del whisked H. Jeanne Walsingham Higgins off to her room, amid a chorus of highly extravagant adjectives with which each seemed to be trying to deafen the other. Polly had seen enough to convince her that the red hair was redder than her's, but she had not decided whether that fact was consoling or not, when Syd appeared, coming across the lawn, whistling nonchalantly, with his cap on the back of his head, and his hands in his pockets.

"Yes, I have seen my grandfather," he replied, somewhat shortly, to Aunt Katherine's inquiry, "and I've had all the breakfast I want—a lobster and some cheese down on the wharf." ("Oh, boys!" groaned Kate, while Polly had a vague but comforting feeling that a boy must have a conscience at ease to relish such a breakfast as that.)

"What are you staring at a feller like that for, Polly? Your eyes are big enough and round enough, anyhow, without making saucers of them," said Syd, crossly. And he went by her, still whistling, around the corner of the house, towards the old wing.

Polly wished very much to follow him, and try to discover the nature of his interview with his grandfather, but discretion was necessary in getting along with Syd, so she restrained herself, although she strongly suspected that his indifference was affected. There was a look about his face which showed to Polly's practiced eye that something was much amiss with him.

Bess was troubled by no such scruples. As soon as she caught sight of Syd from the

Del and H. Jeanne Walsingham Higgins.

cherry-tree where she was endeavoring to console herself for Polly's crossness—" something sweet in the mouth" would console Bess very speedily—she jumped down and ran after him.

"Oh, Syd, what did grandpa want of you? You must have been doing something dreadful, I know, by the way he looked," she called.

Polly could not hear the answer, if Syd vouchsafed one.

"Polly, if you *could* stop kicking!" said Kate, with a slight trace of irritation.

"Oh, Polly, come and see what Syd is doing!"

Polly thought she might go, but she must not only restrain her tongue, but her eyes.

The windows and shutters of Syd's room in the old wing were thrown wide open, and the curtains were drawn aside, and he was coming from the carriage-house with some paint and a brush.

"Come up! come right up!" said Syd. "You won't have to sneak and spy round here any more!"

"Oh, Syd!" said Polly, reproachfully. She thought he ought to remember her magnanimity about the key, but it was evident that he didn't.

She turned to go back, but anxiety, and no small amount of curiosity mingled with it, were stronger than her pride.

"What an orfle smell!" said Bess, as they entered Syd's room.

"It's like chemistry days at school, and something like a dentist's shop, and—you don't mind, do you, Syd?—a *great deal* like a fishing-smack."

"And cold tobacco-smoke," added Bess.

Polly had perceived that odor, with a shudder, but she had refrained from mentioning it. It would do no good to make Syd angry.

He was vigorously painting out the highly colored device on the door, and took no notice. Bess investigated closets and drawers.

"I don't believe he has had anything here but just common boys' rubbish," she said.

"He only wanted to have a secret. Boys are often silly. When I was very small, Kitty Park and I had a secret, and we made the girls half crazy because we wouldn't tell them; and Daisy Jones cried; and it was only that Kitty was going to marry Dr. Gunsaulus, when she grew up, because he had a monkey. I don't believe Syd's secret would amount to any more than that, if you found it out. It just made him feel important to lock us all out.

"Syd, has any one been arrested for burning grandpa's barn?" asked Polly. One of Polly's great trials was, that she could not keep from saying things which she had firmly resolved not to say.

"Yes, Nick Hiffley," answered Syd, not looking at her, but apparently having great difficulty in painting the door just to his mind. "But he'll be discharged before to-morrow night. I told grandpa so. They can't prove anything."

Polly stared at him with a roundness of the

eyes which he would have found quite unpardonable if he had been looking.

"How do you know?" she said, and her effort at self-control made her voice deep and impressive.

"I do know, and that's enough," said Syd, reddening angrily. "And I know, too—" Syd stopped painting and faced her, and spoke very deliberately—"I know, too, what I think of a girl who is ready to suspect her own brother of the very worst things—"

"Oh, I'm not, I don't! Oh, Syd, I would be so thankful not to!" cried Polly, incoherently, half strangled by the great sob in her throat, which she would hold down, for Syd despised a "cry-baby." "I don't think you have done anything wicked yourself, but you go with those boys who do wicked things."

"I've told you before that a feller sometimes gets into a tight place where he can't help himself, and then it's just like a girl to come nagging and fretting him. Why can't you have a little faith in me?"

"I won't nag at you any more," said Polly, humbly. "I didn't mean to, to-day, but I got so dreadfully worried. There's no one I think so much of, Syd. You were very good to me when we were little, before you began to feel above girls, you know, and we were always together."

"You've always been a pretty good feller yourself, Pollykins, and I think a lot of you now;" Syd put his arm around her, a most unusual demonstration for Syd; "although, of course, I don't care about going with girls now. But I say, old Polly, you mustn't get sentimental and weepy; no feller can stand that. You never used to be like that. And you must have had as good grit, almost, as a boy when you were cast away in that old boat. That was tough!" Syd gave her a really heartsome hug, remembering the acuteness of his suffering, which had surprised himself in those hours of suspense:

"It was different," said Polly, immensely

consoled by the hug. "But I'm not crying, and I will believe you are doing the very best you can. I will never doubt you again, never!"

Syd gave her a long, queer look. Polly did not understand, but afterwards she remembered it. He opened his lips as if to speak, impetuously, but Bess's voice broke in:

"Who is doing the very best he can? I can't say it seems a bit like Syd. Oh, Syd, is this little nickel chain the one that you fastened your gray squirrel with when you carried him in your pocket? I wish you'd give it to me. Why, Syd, your eyes look as red as if you'd been—"

"Go away, Bess! take anything you want, only go! What if my eyes do look red? I've been out in the sun. Maybe you think I've been crying, like a girl!" said Syd, savagely.

"That's the third time this morning that people have told me to go away, and I sha'n't do it," said Bess, indignantly.

"You'd better both go, and tell Roy that

he can get the glass set in his private entrance, because he won't need to use it any more," said Syd. And as it was evident that no softening of his mood could be expected after he had been suspected of shedding tears, Polly went, and Bess decided to follow her.

"What were you and Syd talking about?" asked Bess. "I'm sorry I stayed so long with those old traps and things; there was nothing new except some bottles of queer stuff as black as ink. I thought I could find out what he and Bruce Bennett had been doing there, but I couldn't. Did he tell you anything? I *knew* he had been crying, I saw tears in his eyes, but of course I had more tact than to say so."

(Perhaps it was from having been long advised to cultivate that quality that Bess had come to fancy herself possessed of a great amount of tact.)

Polly listened absently. She was wishing that Bess had not interrupted them in that softened mood of Syd's, which was so unusual. Ordinarily Syd made one feel that he had hidden his real self away under lock and key; there was no getting at him. And the bottles of "queer stuff, as black as ink," which Bess had seen reminded her of the strange, bubbling sound which Roy and she had heard in that room; that sound was always connected, vaguely, in her mind with the three witches in Macbeth, with their cauldron and their "double, double, toil and trouble;" she had seen them at the theatre when she visited her Aunt Augusta in New York.

But, on the whole, she was greatly relieved. Syd had looked so honest and true, and she was firmly resolved to keep her word, and to believe in him, although appearances might be against him.

As they went around the house—Bess, with ruffled dignity which Polly was too absent-minded to soothe—they saw the dingy old steamboat carriage with its antiquated steed again standing at the door, and from it was alighting, with difficulty, a little elderly lady, with a very large nose, and a pair of sharp, twinkling black eyes.

"Oh, horrors! it's Aunt Augusta," gasped Del, who was peeping through the closed blinds. "She has swooped down to see what we're up to."

"Eh? what? Why does it matter that I came in the hired carriage? I'm not a sugar-toy of a woman that a little jolting should put me in danger," said Aunt Augusta, in answer to the exclamations that greeted her. "It was weary waiting, but a bit of a thing that was all fuss and feathers hired the carriage before me, and when she and her airs were in, what room was there for a plain, decent body like me?"

Aunt Augusta *was* plain in respect of her dress, which was of gray homespun, short and scanty, and altogether unfashionable in make; but she wore a large amount of crisply curled false hair, and her hands, only partially concealed by lace mitts, were shining with rings.

"I do wish we might have had some one who is a credit to us just now! Aunt Augusta is a thing of shreds and patches," said Del, disrespectfully, after Aunt Augusta had retired to her room to repair the ravages of travel. "I think it must be the Scotch blood, of which she is always boasting, that makes her so thrifty that she won't buy anything to wear except jewels that are always valuable. Her diamonds are superb; *Jeanne* will admire those; but if she went to an elegant reception she'd be sure to leave them at home, and she always wears them in travelling, because she feels safer about them. I don't suppose she ever goes anywhere, however, except to industrial homes and orphan asylums. With all her money, and as many different countries as she has lived in, she ought to know somebody. She might be of use to us." Del's last clause was added in an aggrieved tone.

Roy and Lord Brentford appeared in the doorway at that moment, and Del perceived, somewhat to her discomfiture, that they must have overheard her. But Del never meant that any one should see that she was discomfited; she generally tried to conceal it by being flippant and talking at random.

"You are having a great opportunity to see queer Americans," she said, turning to the young lord. "The very queerest one of us is here now! I only wish Kenneth had come too; he is her son. He is a little fellow, with a turn-up nose, and he carries his head in the air, and is frightfully conceited; says rude things to everybody. Polly always took to him, and *she* calls it being frank. He snubbed her dreadfully too. She used to invite him to go everywhere last summer, when he was here, and get up parties on purpose for him, because the rest of us couldn't bear him and she thought he was sensitive about it; and he told me he *had* to snub Polly because she tried to superintend his movements; he couldn't have any girl ordering him about."

"What a puppy!" exclaimed Lord Brentford.

"Isn't he? And Polly will like him still. She says he cares for peoples' rights, if he doesn't for their feelings, and he will do, at any sacrifice, what he believes to be right."

Polly thought the English boy must be thinking about setting down this example of an American boy's conceit, in his note-book, but he looked at her very gravely, and remarked:

"I think Miss Polly is inclined to believe in people always, and see only the best in them. It's a beautiful trait, but I'm afraid it isn't always wise or safe."

It sounded as if he knew about Syd. Polly's heart beat quickly under his serious gaze. But how could he know? She had no time to think now, for Del's friend appeared, radiant in a stylish costume, and grown-up airs and graces, and monopolized the conversation with a history of her journey.

"There was the very funniest little old frump of a woman on the steamer!" she said. "Her clothes must have come out of the ark, and she had the queerest topknot of a wig, and she was knitting all the way on a great long stocking, and fancy! she wore as many diamonds as if she were going to a ball. I suppose they were paste."

Even airy little Jeanne Higgins shrank back in dismay as, from a remote corner of the room, dressed in an ancient black satin, short and skimpy, but so stiff that it set out around her like a balloon, Aunt Augusta bore rapidly down upon her.

CHAPTER XIV.

H. JEANNE HIGGINS, although she shrank from the threatening danger, bore the shock very well when it came. Aunt Augusta stood directly before her, and gazed at her steadfastly, with her little, piercing black eyes, and the girl arose with a pretty little air of deference, and looking calm, although her cheeks blazed.

"Introduce your friend to me, Delphine," she said. "I have a word to say to her, and I wouldn't be unmindful of etiquette, for I'll be bound she thinks a deal of it. Indeed, I have a good opinion of it myself, as a preserver of the decencies of life. Little girl, for ye *are* a little girl, though I've no doubt ye think yourself a young lady," she continued, impressively, after Del had duly presented her friend, "there are, no doubt, a deal of things that ye have to learn, but there's one thing in parteecular"— Aunt Augusta always showed her Scotch blood in her speech when she became excited —"one thing in parteecular that ye'll do well to take great pains to learn, for many a one goes to his grave in ignorance of it, and that's the difference between paste and diamonds. Ye may say what ye like about the old frump ye saw in the boat—perhaps she struck ye no worse than she was struck by ye—but take heed that ye learn the difference between paste and diamonds. And now who's the strange boy?"

Del made the presentation with alacrity, thankful that Jeanne had escaped so easily.

"So you are an English boy, and a lord? Well, an English boy is me cousin, whoever he may be, and ye've a fine, honest countenance!" And Aunt Augusta imprinted a kiss upon Lord Brentford's blushing brow. "And how are ye all behaving with the father and mother gone?

I promised meself a peep without giving any warning. 'When the cat's away the mice will play.'" Aunt Augusta seated herself with no further sign of displeasure against Jeanne Higgins than a slight turning of her back upon her. "And the papers are full of stories of the evil doings of the strikers—rioting, and burning buildings, and making disturbances generally. With all that and ye too upon his hands ye're grandfather must be driven daft!"

"Oh, we never make grandpa any trouble. We take care of him," said Kate, innocently. And Polly almost envied Kate those pretty soft blue eyes of hers, which never discovered anything disagreeable.

"But these troubles worry him very much," continued Kate. He looked more careworn to-day than I ever saw him. I have been thinking that a party of us ought to drive out to The Bend and cheer him up."

The plan met with great favor. Every one wished to go, that afternoon—every one except Syd, who had a previous engagement. Syd seldom went anywhere with the others now, but had Bruce Bennett as an inseparable companion. It was understood that Kate was to go with the two aunts in the family carriage, Del was to drive her friend and the two boys in the phaeton, and Polly and Bess were relegated to Carrots and the donkey cart. But when they were ready to set out, it appeared that the young lord had set his heart upon the donkey cart, and as Carrots frantically took the lead, after his inevitable habit, he and Roy were discovered seated in the back, in high glee, with their legs dangling out.

"I'm afraid it wasn't polite," said Lord Brentford, "but I don't know how to get on with young ladies yet. And she is *such* a howler! I'm more afraid of her than of your sister."

Del was very much discomfited.

"He is rude, if he is English," she said. "Although I can't say that he has ever been so before."

"I consider it very rude," said Jeanne; "but who cares about a boy like that, since his being a lord won't signify where we are going?"

"I have a great big paper of caramels in my pocket," said Del.

"Put them right here on the seat between us! There is nothing much better than caramels," said Jeanne, heartily, taking off one of the lemon-colored kid gloves which just matched her dress.

Carrots was in one of his best humors, and Bose, who had chosen to cast his fortunes in with the cart, had challenged him to a race, and the donkey cart was quite out of sight of its followers before they were out of the village.

"I'm glad that bobbing, clattering thing is out of the way," said Jeanne Higgins. "A donkey cart is so childish! How ridiculous those great boys are in it!"

Del assented, but she heaved a little sigh.

She couldn't help remembering what good times she had had in that donkey cart. Sometimes it did seem, as Polly often told her, a mistake to try to be grown-up so soon.

The day was bright and beautiful, with a cool breeze to temper the July heat, and the pony, though fat, was lively. They drove along a wide street, shaded by great elms, whose branches met above their heads; there were smooth lawns and pretty flower-gardens on either hand, and the houses, although modest in architecture, were cheerful and home-like; and flashing through the trees came glimpses of bright blue water.

Jeanne found the houses "hideous" or "ugly *a faire peur*," or "impossible." "Oh, but that's the Wheelocks; such good times as we have had there!" said Del. "I always thought— of course until I knew better—that it was a beautiful house; and that's the Clarkson's; we thought so much of little Betty who died; and that's the Burbanks. Oh, I suppose it is an ugly house, but such an attic as they have, with great trunks full of elegant old things to dress up in, and such a hall for a dance, or a rainy-day romp; and there are ten children, and oh, when they're all at home it's delightful!—or I used to think so; I don't know that I should like it now. I wonder if they know it's an ugly house; they think so much of their home," she added, meditatively.

"I suppose they're—you won't mind my saying it, if they *are* your friends?—rather common people," said Jeanne.

"Yes, I suppose they are," said Del, doubtfully. "They've never been abroad, or even to Newport, and I'm not sure that they ever heard of Tuxedo. The boys will go to Bowdoin, and the girls to Bates, or perhaps up to Wellesley, and if they ever go abroad it will be to study. Jack is wild over a violin, and Mary paints very well; Ruth wants to be a doctor, and Nan declares she will be a nurse."

"Horrors!" ejaculated Jeanne.

"Well, she was born so," said Del, apologetically. "She used to keep a hospital for sick dolls when she was little, and she has been nursing all the poor and sick old women in town ever since she's worn long dresses. And there's Horace, he won't be a lawyer, like his father, because he knows he can be a better mechanic. Ashamed? Oh, no, they're not ashamed of *anything* of that kind. They are very hospitable, and they're the life of everything about here; but I don't think they would ever be likely to get into society."

"It's a great pity, for I suppose they have some money."

"Oh, yes; not a great deal, for so many, but by pinching in some ways they might live much more fashionably."

"Some people have so little ambition," sighed Jennie.

"But I do like the Burbanks," said Del, loyally; "they will do anything for other people. They think so much of helping everybody, especially poor and lonesome people, if it is only to a good time."

Jeanne looked somewhat contemptuous.

"Queer, 'cranky' people, aren't they?" she said. "I should think one might have good enough times here when one is a little girl, but it must be dreadful to live here when one gets old enough to come out. And you haven't any one to ask you about, have you?"

"We don't seem to know any one who is really in society," said Del, sorrowfully. "Mamma is so much of an invalid, and papa cares for nothing but his horrid old scientific books."

"I shall look out for you, if I can; of course it will be difficult, but we know every one," said Jeanne, grandly.

"Oh, Jeanne, if you only will!" exclaimed Del, eagerly. "If I only could once go somewhere where things are different from Green Harbor!"

"Of course it isn't easy to get invitations for a visit for a stranger," said Jeanne; "and, besides, there are some places where if one isn't out, one is kept in the background, so that it is only an aggravation; but I know some houses where there are no young girls, and they like to have them, and they'll bring you forward. Mamma doesn't mind, she likes it; she'd bring me out only she thinks people would talk."

They were driving through a beautiful woods road now, soft birds' notes and drowsy insect hummings mingled harmoniously with the gentle rustling of the leaves, and every breath was sweet with the fragrance of the fir-trees and the innumerable delicious scents of the woods; and those girls, Jeanne occupied with her little vain boasts, and Del with her forehead puckered with anxiety, were unconscious of it all. A squirrel, all bright eyes and bushy tail, that had rushed along the fence beside them, looking and listening, suddenly darted off with a great chattering to his friend in the top of a tall pine-tree, and I have every reason to believe that what he said to his friend was, "Oh, how silly girls can be, and how much more sense we squirrels have!"

I am glad to tell what happened afterwards, although Jeanne said she was really so dreadfully mortified that she should never get over it.

They turned from the woods road into a broad, smooth turnpike, and The Bend was in sight. A great white house, ancient and homelike, under sheltering elms, stood on a knoll, surrounded by orchards and gardens and fields of grass and grain. A little river, a tributary of the Penobscot, made a sharp turn behind the orchard, and, wandering away among the fields, reappeared in front of the house; it looked from the spot where the girls came in sight of it like a tiny band of blue ribbon.

"Why, it looks like an ordinary farmhouse!" said Jeanne; "but of course it has been in the family for generations, and that makes a difference."

"Oh, no—" began Del, with an honest impulse, but paused suddenly. How stupid it would be of her to confess that grandpa was born in that little, old, tumble-down, one-story house on the other side of the river, near the mill, and that his father was the miller! She had already told her about grandma, who was of aristocratic Huguenot descent, and had inherited some priceless china and the smallest hands and feet in the state.

As they turned in at the great gates, and drove along beside the orchard wall, Jeanne caught sight of something which made her forget, for the moment, all social concerns.

"Oh, what great *big* cherries!" she cried. "And see, at the very top of the tree they're ripe!"

"That's the black-heart tree; they're the

most delicious cherries! I didn't think they had begun to ripen yet."

"Aren't any of the servants about? Can't they get us some?" asked Jeanne.

"The men are all haying down in that field, I think, Aaron and all. Aaron manages the farm; he lives in that little house, all by himself; he won't have a woman to do his work, and you should see him knitting his stockings and darning his clothes!" Del was preparing to drive on.

"I *must* have some of those cherries! The donkey cart is fastened over there by the house, isn't it? And there comes the carriage. Just wait a minute, and let them pass; they'll think we want to let the pony eat some of this clover. Now, Del"—as the carriage drove by—"there's a long ladder, and I'm going to get some of those cherries."

"You'll spoil yourself," said Del, regarding Jeanne's elegant attire and her own white gown doubtfully, yet with a lingering look at the cherries.

"We can pin up our dresses." Jeanne hopped over the wall, and Del followed, leaving the fat pony contentedly munching the clover.

The long ladder was heavy, but their combined exertions soon placed it in proper position, and up they both went.

"We have got to go beyond the ladder, away, way up into the tree. I believe this is the very tallest cherry-tree that ever was! There are none ripe on the lower branches, except out at the very end where we can't get them," said Del.

"Never mind! it's great fun. Go on!" said Jeanne.

"Oh, Jeanne, aren't they lovely? And such a lot!" was the next remark. "I wish we had something to put them into."

"I'm sufficiently provided," said Jeanne, with her mouth full.

"There are more up here! Oh, bushels! but I've scratched my face dreadfully," said Del.

"Never mind! I've torn a great lock of hair out by the roots, and it's *all* hanging down, but I do love to be up in a tree! I'm afraid I shall never get over liking it— Oh—oh, dear! Oh! Oh!"

A great crashing accompanied Jeanne's exclamations.

"Oh, what *is* the matter? have you slipped?" cried Del.

"The branch broke that I was standing on! I'm clinging to another, but my foot is caught in a crotch, and I *can't* get it out. Come quick, and see if you can!"

In the haste of her descent Del hit the ladder, and down to the ground it fell with a crash.

"Oh, Jeanne, the ladder is gone, and I can't get to you! There's no way, now that limb is broken! Oh, what *shall* we do? I must call for help!"

"Don't you do it! I'll never forgive you if you do! I should *die* of shame to be caught in such a ridiculous plight."

Some frantic wrigglings on Jeanne's part followed these words.

"Oh! oh, dear! I can't get my foot out, and it's beginning to hurt, and my hair is all twisted into a branch and pulls dreadfully."

"And I can't get a good foothold, and it's frightfully slippery here. And it seems so high now the ladder is gone! What *shall* I do?"

"*Holler!*" said Jeanne, desperately.

CHAPTER XV.

DEL lifted up her voice vigorously in obedience to Jeanne's injunction, but for a time there was no response, except from the robins flying above their heads, who had been defrauded of their feast, and were apparently rejoicing over the misfortunes which had befallen those queer creatures who, clearly, had no business to be in a cherry-tree.

It was Aaron who came to the rescue, at length; a keen, dry old man, with a face like a baked apple, and a smooth and shining bald head which formed a curious contrast to it.

"Who *be* you, a-screechin' up top of that tree? I declare if it ain't a parcel of girls! I don't allow nobody up there. As if them sassy robins wa'n't tormentin' enough!" grumbled Aaron.

"Put the ladder up, quick, and come up and help us, Aaron! Be quick!" cried Del.

"Well, if it ain't some of our own youngsters! Is that you, Del? Beats all nater how you ever got up so high! Who is the other little gal? I thought, fust off, 'twas our Polly, but I snum if it ain't a redder head than her'n!"

"Aaron, *will* you hurry?" cried Del.

"I should like to know how I'm a-goin' to hurry when you've broke the ladder!" said Aaron. "Here's one side of it split clean in two, and I snum if it ain't the only one we've got, for the other two, the little one and the middlin'-sized one, was burnt up in the barn."

"Oh, what shall we do? Tell him to get us down, some way, directly," said Jeanne.

"Well, what be I goin' to do?" demanded Aaron, scratching his head, in great perplexity. "Gals hadn't ought to climb trees; it's agin nater," he added, as if that fact relieved him from all responsibility. "I don't expect you can hold on, neither; women folks can't. You'll be a-tumblin' down here and breakin' your necks, next thing, and the guv'nor 'll lay it to *me*. There comes the boys, Roy and that outlandish youngster. If ever I was glad to see boys! Here boys, there's a couple of gals up top of that cherry-tree, and the ladder's broke, and they're consid'able broke up, themselves, and you've got to contrive some way to git 'em down."

Roy went up the tree like a squirrel. One good thing about Roy was that he never stopped to talk in an emergency, and he soon released Jeanne's foot from its uncomfortable imprisonment, while Lord Brentford, after ascertaining that the nearest house was too far away to make it practicable to go there for a ladder, got to work to "splice" the ladder, which he did in a most workmanlike manner.

"Now you see there are only two rounds that it won't do to step on. By skipping those they can come down safely," he said.

"They can't skip nothin'. Gals never can," growled Aaron.

But in spite of Aaron's scepticism they did skip the rounds and came safely down, none the worse, except for Jeanne's slight lameness, a somewhat soiled and draggled appearance, and a great loss of dignity. Lord Brentford privately confided to Roy that he liked that girl much better when her " toggery " was all spoiled, and he thought her hair pretty when it wasn't all stuck up in little knobs and frizzled into her eyes like a Skye's. Roy didn't think much of girls anyway; he only remarked, " Didn't she holler, though ?" and that he had picked up about a quart of hairpins under the tree; he supposed she would want them, but he didn't exactly like to give them to her. He ungraciously added, after a few moments' reflection, that he hoped she would go home soon; Del could be silly enough without *her*.

Lord Brentford took out his note-book, and, resting it upon the orchard wall, he set down his somewhat revised opinions of Miss H. Jeanne Walsingham Higgins. His lordship's notes on American girls bade fair to rival those on American insects, although his study of the latter, and natural history in general, had become so interesting with Roy's companionship that he had persuaded his tutor, who was convalescent, to take up his quarters at the Green Harbor hotel for the summer. He added some notes about Polly, with slightly wrinkled brows, for Roy had confided to him something of the trouble about Syd which gave a clew to Polly's conduct. He still recorded his impression that, although probably not a revolutionist, she was far too independent, and inclined to meddle with things not fit for girls, and ought really to have a governess or be sent away to school.

He added some reflections on the strikers, who were dealt with far too leniently; and on the disturbed state of the town, which would not be tolerated in England for a moment. And he finished with some very sage doubts as to the practicability of a republican form of government.

And then he suddenly decided that it was not the part of an Englishman to be afraid of any girl, and resolved to go and talk to Miss Jeanne Higgins.

Roy, who had been lying on his back, on the orchard grass, looking at the shifting clouds through the tree-tops, and, no doubt, making philosophical reflections on the universe, made no objection to having this occupation interrupted, and they went into the house. There was no mug of cider on the back porch, but there was a lunch spread in the great, cool hall which ran through the house. There was buttermilk, which Aunt Augusta had ordered, and coffee and cream for more ordinary tastes, cold chicken, and daintiest pink ham, and great yellow bowls full of strawberries; and grandpa was full of kindly, if not elegant, hospitality.

Lord Brentford found an opportunity to place himself beside Jeanne Higgins. He produced some Indian arrow-heads from his pocket.

"These are very curious and interesting, remarkably so," he said; "but, do you know, if it hadn't been for the Indians I don't see what you would have done for relics."

"*Relics?*" cried Jeanne, fixing him with her bright brown eyes. "If there's anything we *don't* want it's relics!" What a queer boy you are!"

And she turned her back upon him so far as circumstances would allow. He felt, as he afterwards explained to Roy, "utterly crushed."

"I shouldn't have said such an idiotic thing if she hadn't got her hair done up again!

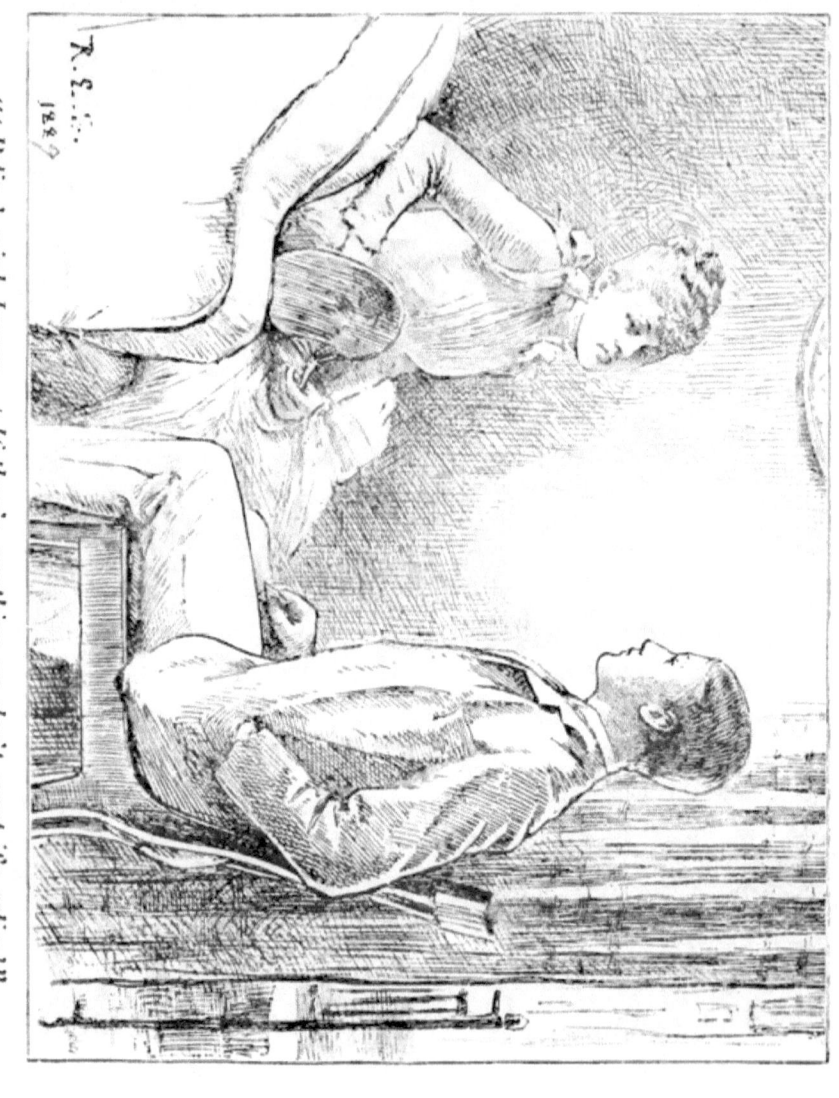

"'Relics,' cried Jeanne. 'If there's anything we don't want it's relics.'"

When it was down her back she seemed jolly, and as if a fellow could talk to her, you know."

He tried to restore his self-complacency by talking to Polly. One could be even a little condescending to Polly, who had not thought of beginning to be a young lady. Jeanne confided her impressions of him to Del at the first opportunity.

"Slangy boys one gets used to," she said, "and dandy boys, and even boys who try to be fast, but a relicky boy, with a note-book, I never met before. And he doesn't seem to have an idea that he is doing anything rude in openly putting people down in his book. I should like to know how he has put me down! He looks at me solemnly and disapprovingly. I think he is disappointed that I'm not a relic!"

"But he wasn't stupid about the ladder," said Del, candidly.

Meanwhile the English boy was walking

with Polly to the ruins of the barn. He had never taken any notice of her before; she was always classed with the children, and no one was expected to. Polly was not quite sure that Del would like it, although she had become quite disgusted with his lordship for being too young and too "buggy"—the irreverent way in which she referred to his entomological pursuits.

Polly thought it very kind of him to come with her, but afterwards she wished that he hadn't.

The work of removing the ruins of the burned barn was to be begun the next day, and as they looked up at the few remaining blackened timbers and recalled mournfully the good times they had had there, grandpa assured them, although with a cheerfulness that seemed a little forced, that they should have the husking frolic just the same as usual, and Aaron would play "Come, lasses and lads," and all the old dancing tunes, all the better in a brand-new barn. But Aaron, who was inclined to gloomy views, said, "With such goin's on as there was now it looked more as if they should be all burned in their beds before that time." And Aunt Augusta sat down on one end of a blackened log, which Aaron gallantly covered with his coat, and he sat upon the other end, and they discussed labor and capital, apparently on terms of perfect equality, except that Aaron was a trifle condescending to Aunt Augusta's limited womanly capacity. Lord Brentford felt for his note-book, but gave it up with a great sigh, as if he found the country an unsolvable problem.

He followed Polly, who was tiptoeing over some planks of the flooring which remained. She stooped suddenly and picked up something from a heap of debris.

"A knife!" said Lord Brentford. "Do you know whose it is? It may be a clew to the discovery of the incendiary," he added, eagerly.

"Why, it's—" Polly stopped, turning a pale and startled face towards him.

"Yes, I know whose it is," she said, shortly, "but it doesn't belong to any one who—who set the fire."

"She is trying to shield some one—a child like that!" said Lord Brentford to himself. "What a miserable business! She has taken it into her head to sympathize with the strikers; she thinks she's a young Joan of Arc! This can't be for her brother's sake. Good heavens! it isn't possible that he is mixed up with a thing like this, is it? I'm not sure but it is my duty to tell about the knife. But I'll wait and see what happens. I don't much like the appearance of Master Syd. He is sulky and keeps himself to himself in a way that is suspicious. And I haven't forgotten how guilty he looked about the cutting of that rope that came so near to drowning Polly. What a little fool she is! The best thing that can happen to a rogue is to be caught.

I wonder what the grandfather can be thinking of, if he has any suspicions. They're an easy lot of people! Fancy youngsters left to themselves like this! I'll wait awhile; I don't want to have anything to do with it, but if I think it is my duty—"

He drew his boyish figure up very straight, with this reflection, and Polly half guessed what was passing in his mind.

"Lord Brentford, you won't tell? You have no right to tell, without my leave, that I have found anything here." In spite of the authoritative tone Polly's voice faltered.

"You don't seem to see that the very fact that you wish me not to, makes me feel that it is my duty to. No one who has been guilty of such a crime ought to be screened," he said, with a judicial air.

"The owner of the knife will tell me whether he had anything to do with it," said Polly. "He will tell me the truth. I am quite sure he will. We have made a compact. I sha'n't try to screen him, as you say; if he has done it, I shall tell grandpa."

"Wouldn't it be better—excuse me, Miss Polly, but I think it would be much better to tell your grandfather at once. Under such circumstances the most truthful person—"

"He isn't a truthful person at all," said Polly, sadly. "He is perfectly notorious for telling lies. But he won't tell me one. He may not own up, you know, he is so unused to owning up; but if he did it he won't tell me that he didn't."

"It can't be her brother; she wouldn't say such things about him! It may be the friend who wrote to her 'Bewar you ar wotched.' What a country! One expects to find the babies with cartridge-boxes for rattles and the small girls experimenting with dynamite. And yet"—Lord Brentford seemed struck by a wholly new idea—"perhaps the whole country isn't just like Green Harbor. Well, I should like to save little Miss Polly from being blown up, if I can't save her from burning her fingers."

"I hope your confidence may not prove to be misplaced," he said, stiffly, and Polly read a world of disapprobation in his tone.

She could hardly contain herself until she reached home; it seemed as if the others would stay forever, on one pretext or another, and then Carrots became a perfect imp of perversity; he backed them up against a stone wall, and almost over it, and he had to be cajoled all the way home by means of green apples held before him. The lively exertions necessary were performed in turn by Roy and Lord Brentford, and they consumed much time. Polly slipped out of the cart just before they reached Birch Point. She had discovered, in spite of the gathering darkness, a long, angular figure with coat-tails, whittling and whistling cheerfully, upon a fence.

"Cainy," began Polly, solemnly; and then

she suddenly reflected that it might be better to stoop to a little artifice. "Let me take your knife a minute."

"This is Billy Rundlett's knife; it ain't no good," said Cainy.

"Where's yours? the one that Harry gave you last Christmas?"

"I lent it to Syd, more'n two weeks ago, and he hain't give it back," said Cainy, in an aggrieved tone. "I asked him for it—how's a feller goin' to git along when he can't cut nothin'?—but he said he'd mislaid it. He looked kind of red and mad 'cause I asked him, but 'twas a three-blader 'n' a gimlet 'n' a file, that knife was, and I ain't a-goin' to be sot on."

CHAPTER XVI.

To Polly's straightforward nature there seemed but one course to pursue. She went directly in search of Syd to ask him how he had lost Cainy's knife. It cannot be claimed that Polly was shrewd, or even wise; but wisdom does not make itself thoroughly at home in thirteen-year-old heads. Lord Brentford's advice was unquestionably good. Her grandfather was a fitter person to deal with the matter than she. But Polly had a feeling that no one else understood Syd even as well as she did, and grandpa, easy-going and careless up to a certain point, could be stern, even harsh, when that point was passed. And Syd's faults were of the kind with which grandpa had least patience. He had always been inclined to be harder upon Syd than upon any of the others.

Moreover, Syd had such a fatal tendency to be sly and evasive; it seemed impossible for him to face any difficulty or any accusation squarely, even though it might be greatly to his advantage to do so. He would be very likely to make people think him guilty even if he were not.

Polly was quite convinced that it was not her duty to tell of Syd until she was sure that he was guilty. The finding of Cainy's knife in the ruins of the barn had seemed to her almost positive proof that Cainy had been among the incendiaries, but when the responsibility for the knife came upon Syd the matter had a different aspect. Cainy was not approved of at The Bend, and Aaron was vigilant in keeping boys out of the barn, but Syd might have lost the knife there before the night of the fire.

Polly sought for Syd that night in vain; he was not at home, and she found no opportunity to speak to him. She was tempted to go to his room after he had gone to bed and speak to him through the keyhole, but Syd was inclined to be cross when he was sleepy, and, besides, she would be at a disadvantage, for Syd's face often told more than his words; and there was the danger that others might hear. She resolved to wait, but—poor Polly!—the suspense was hard to bear; and she dreamed that Syd was going to be hanged upon a limb of the black-heart cherry-tree, where Del and her friend had been made captives, and Aunt Augusta was to be hanged also, for sympathizing with the strikers, and she, with full proof of their innocence in her hands, was sailing, against the wind, in the old *High-Flyer*, and could not get to land in time to save them. And then, suddenly, the victim of the execution changed to Carrots, and Polly awoke just as she was trying to resign herself to Carrots' fate on the ground that he richly deserved it.

Polly might have come to the same decision that she did without this ridiculous dream, but I am inclined to think that its horrors influenced her.

She arose early and found Syd in the upper story of the stable, repairing his pigeon-house, which had fallen to wreck and ruin since his absorption in the companionship of Bruce Bennett and in mysterious societies. This return to peaceful every-day avocations struck Polly as a hopeful sign. A Red-Handed Revolutionist, intent upon " slaying, burning, and destroying," seemed unlikely to trouble himself about pigeons.

She went up the stairs until her chin was on a level with the floor; boards and tools and shavings made it impracticable to go farther.

"Syd, what did you do with Cainy's knife? Did you lend it to anybody?" (This was one of the hopes which Polly had cherished.)

"Cainy's knife? So he has been complaining to you, has he? Well, if he isn't a sneak! When I've given him as many as a dozen knives, with only one broken blade, too!"

Syd was measuring laths; he did not stop nor turn his head.

"Did you lose it, Syd?" Polly's voice trembled.

"What is that to you?" said Syd, facing her suddenly.

"I have found it, Syd. I found it in the ruins of grandpa's barn."

"Oh, you did, did you? And what if you did? Oh, you've got some more of your suspicions have you? That's as much as I supposed your promise would amount to! Give it here!" Syd extended his hand for the knife, and Polly gave it to him.

"I haven't said that I didn't believe in you, Syd. I haven't *acted* as if I didn't. I brought it to you when I might have carried it to grandpa, instead. I haven't told any one.

Lord Brentford saw me pick it up, and he said it might be a clew."

"Oh, he did! Well, with the British aristocracy to back you, I dare say you'll enjoy getting me into hot water!"

Polly felt her temper tottering to its fall, and she resorted to the only expedient that ever availed her in that extremity; she ran away. Bess could count a hundred and feel, as she said, "hardly mad at all" at the end of it, and Del said she kept in by reflecting that people who would stoop to say hateful things were not worth noticing; but Polly *had* to run away.

She ran no farther this time than to the stable door, where she sat down upon an inverted pail. There was a bare possibility that Syd might relent and come to seek her; that had happened, although but seldom.

Although Syd was so provoking and Polly often became very angry with him, her anger never seemed to weaken her affection for him or to take the edge off her anxiety. Perhaps this was because she had a vague but abiding faith that the real, inside Syd was something better than it seemed. Syd was like a chestnut in its burr to Polly's mind—very prickly on the outside; un-get-at-able too, like a green one; but she believed there was a sound, sweet kernel.

Or, if there were not, what could she do but love him and try to help him, since he was her own, and she had begun so early that it was now like the breath she drew? Polly knew that she loved Syd better than any of the others did, and she didn't always like grandpa's ways.

The carelessness of her elders had led Polly to sit in judgment upon them in a way which she vaguely felt to be wrong; perhaps this is done oftener than they realize by thirteen-year-olds who can by no means comprehend the value of the lessons of that grim old teacher Experience. But let us hope that

Polly will not go far wrong, since it is true that Love can often find the way which Wisdom seeks for in vain.

She found a grain of comfort in Syd's crossness, to-day, as his words and looks came back to her. It did not seem to her that he would have behaved just so if he were guilty. Gradually she began to feel that Syd had been almost justified in being cross; she had shown that she doubted instead of trusting him, as she had promised. She almost felt that she ought to beg his pardon, but she would not do that, anyway, for Syd hated it; he called it sentimental and just like a girl, and said if people felt like begging other people's pardons they had better show it by their actions. When they were little she was accustomed to give him something, on such occasions; although he often received it churlishly, Syd was always inwardly mollified by a gift. There was that time when she had gone up to Bangor with grandpa in the sleigh, instead of coaxing grandpa to take him instead, when she knew he wanted particularly to go; and Syd wouldn't make up until she gave him her pug puppy, a gift that made her heart bleed; and then Syd sold the puppy to a man on the steamboat for a dollar! She thought now of giving him her young peacock, whose plumage was beginning to be splendid; he had only a peahen, that was dull and brown; but he might only be angrier still. They were older now, and things were different now that Syd was interested in the conflict between labor and capital, and in reforming the social order.

He was still at work, sawing and hammering, and occasionally he whistled—not like an anarchist, but like any boy, Polly reflected, hopefully; but she waited a long time before he came down.

He passed by her with a scowl of surprise, but without a word; but when he came back, with some nails which he had gone after, he stopped and said, impressively,

"See here, Polly, I'll show you how *men* behave to each other: my grandfather came to me yesterday morning and said right out, squarely, 'Did you have anything to do with setting fire to my barn?' Now of course it's insulting to ask a feller such a question, but this miserable little town is full of gossip, and everything that a feller does is watched and talked about, and made out twice as bad as it is, so I couldn't blame him so very much. He asked me that, and I said, 'No, sir, I didn't.'"

"And then what did grandpa say?" cried Polly, eagerly. To have Syd talk about things straightforwardly like this was like coming out of a fog into brilliant sunlight.

"He said, 'Well, I never knew a Damer to tell a lie.' And then he went off. That's the way with *men;* it takes a girl, and a feller's sister who pretends to like him, at that, to be prying and sneaking and suspicious."

Polly scarcely minded the uncomplimentary terms which, with very strong emphasis, Syd applied to her. She was saying to herself, exultantly, "He didn't do it! He had nothing to do with it, and grandpa knows it!"

Syd was hurrying off, but Polly called him back.

"I don't want you to think, Syd, that I don't understand how you feel about wanting to help the poor people. Grandpa said we might carry some things to poor Mrs. Severance, with her sick children, and Kate and I went, and it was pitiful to see them. I think grandpa is right that we can't understand all about the trouble till we're older; but it seems wicked, sometimes, to just go on having a good time when other people are suffering. It seems as if nothing in the world were of any use but just to help people. I don't think it is right to join with those boys; they don't understand, and they do foolish, wicked things; they only make everything worse. But I do think about the troubles, and when I am grown up I think I shall do nothing but try to help people. I sha'n't care whether I have a good time at all if I can only do that." Polly's small frame trembled with her eagerness.

"Polly! I've found out that it isn't so much fun to try to help people," said Syd. "They want to rule everything, and have you do as they say, and they get you into trouble, and that's all the good it does you. Of course it's stupid being nothing but a common boy, forever going to school and studying things over and over that don't mean much of anything, anyway; and Bruce Bennett wants to go out West to the plains; he thinks he could get to be a cow-boy right off; or else he wants to run away to sea. But, you see, there's the chance that a feller might not like being a cow-boy, after all; and as for going to sea, *I'm* so orfle seasick; and you wouldn't get rid of being ordered round there, I can tell you! Being a boy isn't so much fun as some people think, anyhow."

Polly drew a long sigh. Syd did not understand. He had not cared about the poor people at all, although he had talked as if he had, and had called her selfish; he was still thinking only of himself.

"You won't do any of those foolish things that Bruce Bennett wants you to do?—run away, or anything, will you, Syd? I think it would kill mamma."

"I don't know what I may do if people keep suspecting me and nagging at me as they do," said Syd. "I'm 'like a toad under a harrow' as Aaron says. And such a lot of prigs as there are in that boat club! Fancy fellers in this town thinking they're too good to speak to me! Roy's a heavy feller! I guess I'd associate with fellers that treated my own brother like that! I could have my revenge, if I liked, they'd better believe! The folks in this town had better look out, anyway. They're going to see worse things than they have seen!"

With this prophecy Syd went on his way.

Polly felt tempted to run after him and try to find out what he meant, but she decided that it was useless, and might irritate him. It might be only "bluster," as Roy said; Syd was somewhat given to that.

As Polly went towards the house she met Aaron driving in at the gate with some of the choice early vegetables that grandpa liked to send. There was a great basket of blackheart cherries on the seat beside Aaron.

"Them gals needn't have resked their necks for them cherries; they'd have got 'em anyhow," remarked Aaron. "But I expect it's nat'ral for 'em to take after their grandmother Eve. Is Syd anywheres round? Well, you jest tell him that I can't find his knife anywheres. We was tryin' to cut out a harness that had got ketched between some timbers, that mornin' after the fire, and Syd he lost his knife. I didn't *expect* he'd ever find it amongst that rubbish."

Up the stable stairs flew Polly. "Oh, Syd,

Aaron has told me about your knife. I'm so dreadfully sorry that I was ever afraid, for a minute—"

"Oh, get away," growled Syd. "I'm sick of girls."

CHAPTER XVII.

Polly was hemming kitchen towels, making the sewing-machine go with a great clicking and clattering, when Bess came in, with a bee in her bonnet. Bess was quite apt to have a bee in her bonnet, and it was Polly who was expected to listen to its buzzing.

"What do you think Del is up to, now? Do stop that noise and listen. I can't think what you are doing that for, this lovely morning."

"Diantha wanted them, and I felt just like doing something that I didn't like," said Polly, who looked disconsolate.

"What *is* the matter? You have been quite cross for three or four days." (Cross

"'Oh, get away,' growled Syd. 'I'm sick of girls.'"

signified a lack of spirits in Bess's vocabulary.) "I suppose you have been getting vexed with Syd, as he will hardly speak to you. I wonder that you can be so foolish as to mind *him*. I think brothers are apt to be more disagreeable than any one else. See if you don't think this is very queer; Del and that girl were talking and talking on the piazza, for as much as an hour, and it was all about asking Aunt Augusta to do something, and then Del went up to Aunt Augusta's room and *they* talked and talked. What could those girls want Aunt Augusta to do? I couldn't make out."

"Bess, you should never listen to what people don't intend you to hear," said Polly, reprovingly.

"I should never hear anything if I didn't! They always say, 'go away!'" said Bess, in an aggrieved tone. "I think that girl is going home soon. I hope she is, for she said I would always be roly-poly. I don't think Aunt Augusta will do it for them, anyway, for she doesn't like that girl; she calls her Flibbertigibbet. Hark! I hear Del coming out of Aunt Augusta's room, now. I'm going to see if she will tell me."

But Bess, whose bump of curiosity was, as Diantha said, "bigger than all the rest of her," ran up-stairs only just in time to see Del rush into Jeanne Higgins's room and whirl her round in an ecstatic waltz, crying out, "Oh, she will, Jeanne! Isn't it *elegant?* She will!"

And then the door closed sharply, and Bess sat down on the stairs, and, sad to relate, *chewed* her hat ribbon, a habit of extreme youth only indulged in now in moments of deepest depression.

A story-teller having a better opportunity than Bess to gratify her bump of curiosity, I am able to tell what happened behind Jeanne Higgins's suddenly closed door.

Del opened a small morocco case which she held in her hand and showed a pair of earrings; tiny drops that sparkled and flashed in the sunlight.

Jeanne Higgins clasped her hands in ecstacy.

"Oh, I shall, I really shall, wear diamonds before Rinda McClure has ever thought of such a thing! She'll say they're not the thing for young girls, but that will be only envy. I will wear them to Mrs. Dorrance's lawn-party, and just once more, and then I'll send them back, as carefully as possible. Nobody will ever dream that they're not mine."

"You *will* be careful, won't you, Jeanne?" said Del, a faint shadow of anxiety clouding her delight. "For Aunt Augusta did say some things that were not very nice, and I really can't imagine how she happened to let me have them. If anything should happen to them, I can't think what I should do!"

"Don't worry, dear. Of course I shall take the greatest care of them. I can't understand how you can be so afraid of that ridiculous old woman—(you don't mind my calling her ridiculous, if she is your aunt, do you?" Del had the grace to wince a little)—"because you know she really *is* ridiculous. Of course she would say nasty things; she doesn't like me; but that doesn't matter in the least, since we have got the earrings! It was perfectly lovely of you to ask her, and you may be sure I won't forget my promise. There isn't another *girl, not another girl*, that I would think of asking Aunt Theodora to invite to Lenox, she is so very particular; but she'll be just charmed with you, and I assure you that you will see something very different from Green Harbor society, for once in your life!"

Jeanne went away the next day, her visit being shortened by a letter from her mother, who was to go to Newport sooner than she had previously planned, and the day after that Aunt Augusta, too, took her departure, unexpectedly, as she always came and went.

She kept Del on the steamer, at the imminent risk of being carried away, while she charged her, for the twentieth time, to take care of her diamonds.

"Anybody would think I was daft to let you have them," she said. "I know she's not fit to be trusted with them; when she's spreading her tail feathers and thinking of nothing but the eyes of people, she's likely to lose her head altogether. I don't trust *her;* it's you that are responsible for them. Now mind that she doesn't keep them a day longer than was agreed upon, and that she takes the precautions I told you about when they're sent back. See that you write to her, now, the minute you get home. I'm sure I think I was crazy—"

Del had only just time to hop off the plank before it was taken away, and then Aunt Augusta came to the side of the boat, and called out something to her which she did not understand, but which she was very much afraid the others would hear. Kate was foolishly particular about borrowing things, she thought, and Aunt Katherine would by no means have approved of the transaction. She said to herself that she was almost sorry she had done it, Aunt Augusta had made such a fuss; but she was safely off in the steamer, now, and soon she would have her diamonds again, and there was the prospective visit to Lenox, which would pay her for all. If only Jeanne didn't forget her promise! The girls at school accused her of being inclined to forgetfulness, but she had made a great many assurances about this promise, and Del didn't mean to hesitate about putting her in mind of it if necessary.

Lord Brentford and Roy, with the former's tutor, Mr. Meredith, had gone on a trip to Moosehead Lake and Mt. Katahdin, and now that Aunt Augusta and Jeanne Higgins had also left, the house seemed very quiet and deserted. Some cousins from Portland had planned to visit them at this time, but Del had put them off, as she wished to devote all her time to a dressmaker in preparation for her visit to Lenox in September. She even had it in mind to ask grandpa to give her some diamond earrings for this great event. He would by no means understand its importance. He seemed to really think her still a little girl, and he would make fun of her for wanting diamonds, but he might be coaxed into it. A great deal could be done with grandpa if he were taken in the right mood. Aunt Katherine could be sympathetic about a good time, but not about fashionable longings, and she was continually telling her that she did not know how much she was missing by trying to be grown-up too soon.

Grandpa had been in a cheerful mood. The disturbances in the town had ceased; he said that the men were coming to their senses, and talked hopefully of a speedy termination of the strike, when suddenly the riotous, revengeful spirit cropped out again, the fiercer for having been curbed. Fires were set, and stores were robbed, and wanton mischief of many kinds was constantly perpetrated, and so sly were the perpetrators that they were either never caught, or, as in the case of Nick Hiffley, who had been suspected of setting fire to the barn, nothing could be proven against them.

"There is a gang of boys that is a scourge to this town," grandpa said one day to Polly. "The rascals have some long heads among them, for it is impossible to prove any definite charges against them. They've formed a society with some sort of a villainous compact. Officer Meacham is trying to get the names; if he can, it won't be long before we'll have every one of them in jail. They are young, most of them, I hear, but the more dangerous on that account, for they haven't any sense or reason. Cutting the ropes of the *High-Flyer* was their doing, I've no doubt; I've always suspected that young scoundrel Cainy of having something to do with them. I've never liked the looks of that fellow. Your father ought not to keep him. I've talked to him enough about it. He comes of bad stock; his father was a thief."

"I suppose Cainy might not be bad, for all that," said Polly, rather faintly.

"He might not, but he's very likely to," said grandpa. "That law of inheritance doesn't always hold, for there's that little Bruce Bennett. He has generations of the strictest Puritan uprightness behind him, and he is as full of mischief as an egg is of meat. I've seen him, myself, with those 'patch' boys, apparently one of them. By the way, Polly, Syd has got to be separated from that boy. Folks have begun to hint that he is mixed up with that gang, just on account of his being intimate with that boy." Grandpa perused Polly's face attentively. "I don't think there is anything *bad* about Syd, but he's hard to manage. He takes out of kin in being sly and underhanded. He had better be sent away to school, this fall, if there isn't any other way of keeping him away from young Bennett. I've come to that, Polly—" grandpa's strong voice shook—"I've come to that, that there wouldn't be any comfort for me in living if one of you children should go wrong. And I can't trust Syd as I can the rest of you."

A strong impulse, which she had often combated before, seized Polly, to tell her grandfather all that she knew about that foolish, dreadful society; it might be her duty to do so; she might have prevented much of the harm that had been done by them if she had told before. But her old feeling about the sacredness of a promise was strong; she could not believe that a bad promise was better broken than kept; and, besides, she felt that if open disgrace should come to Syd, it would start him on a downward course in which he could not be stopped.

"You must look out for Syd," said grand-

pa, as if answering her thought. "They say
you're Captain Polly. And you and he used
to be greater chums than any of the others."

"*Used to*, grandpa; he feels above girls,
now," said Polly, sadly. "I'm going to do the
best I can, but it is so hard to know how,
sometimes."

Aaron came in search of grandpa just then,
and the opportunity to tell was gone. Polly
felt, as she had often done, as if she were
guilty of conspiring with the R. R. R.'s, and
she wished that she had disregarded her
promise as soon as she could, and told grandpa
all about it. But she soon forgot that
wish in the paralyzing recollection that Officer
Meacham might discover all the members of
the society, and then what would become of
Syd? It is doubtful whether Polly could
ever have sacrificed Syd to the common good,
being, as will have been discovered, not at all
a heroine, but only an ordinary thirteen-
year-old girl, brave in physical danger, but

something of a coward for those she loved, and, altogether, far more loving than wise.

While Polly was feeling this new fear for Syd, a trouble had come upon Del which made her cease to care whether she ever "got into society." What seemed so unlikely, after so many cautions, had really happened. Jeanne had lost, or rather mislaid, as she said, one of Aunt Augusta's diamond earrings! After her first letter, in which she had described, enthusiastically, the delights of Mrs. Dorrance's lawn-party, Del had heard nothing for so many days that she felt obliged to write and ask her to return the earrings, more especially as Aunt Augusta had already written that she was expecting them by every mail.

"I am perfectly distressed," wrote Jeanne. "I have mislaid one of the earrings. I'm sure it is not lost, but must be somewhere in the house, but I can't find it! I don't think the settings were what they ought to be, anyway, or it couldn't have come out. I'm sure it could be matched perfectly at Y——'s, in

New York, if I can't find it; and I would pay for it at once, if I could; but, of course, I haven't so much money of my own, and poor mamma couldn't spare it to me at this time of year. But, of course, you can pay for it easily enough, and I will pay you afterwards. I would rather never have a single new dress, or anything, than not to pay for it. I will send them right away if I should find it.

"P. S. Mamma thinks I had better send this one to you so that you can match it at once if you like. I hope your Aunt Augusta won't make a great fuss. Mamma thinks you ought not to have lent them to me; but I won't let her blame you; I tell her just how hard I coaxed you."

"Oh, what shall I do?" cried Del. "They cost three hundred and fifty dollars, a hundred and seventy-five for one. I can't get so much money without telling what it is for, and I can't tell, they would all think it so dreadful! Oh, what *shall* I do?"

CHAPTER XVIII.

DEL was not one to wring her hands and say "What shall I do?" for any length of time. Some sort of action was necessary to her, and she was very apt to act upon her first impulse. Within an hour after the receipt of Jeanne's letter she was mounted upon Jock, the fat pony, riding towards her grandfather's. Jock was the only available horse, and she could not wait, but she felt as if his persistent laziness would drive her frantic. Jock objected to a burden on his back, in any case, and he would do no more than to amble comfortably along, although she coaxed and scolded and whipped; and he occasionally turned his head and gave her a look which was as much as to say, "Don't you know that nothing in the world is worth making such a fuss about?"

But all things come to an end, and even Jock's lazy amble brought up at The Bend.

"I don't know why I should mind it in the least," said Del to herself, as she dismounted, and discovered her grandfather reading his newspaper upon the back piazza. "I am only going to ask him for my own money, and people are not expected to give an account of that."

Del had remembered that she had some money in the Green Harbor bank. It had been placed there for her benefit when she was a baby, and there was an understanding that it was not to be touched until she was of age. Del had scarcely ever thought of it, in her life; she didn't know how much there was, and never having had anything to do with banks she didn't know how she was to get it; but as her grandfather was the president of the bank, she thought it would be necessary to apply to him. If one of the clerks would have given it to her she would have found it much more agreeable; but she was sure neither of them would without consulting her grandfather, every one so persistently refused to look upon her as grown-up. So she had decided to take the bull by the horns, and lose nothing by delay.

"I want to take some of my money out of the bank, grandpa; a hundred and seventy-five dollars. Will you get it for me?" said she, in a nice little matter-of-fact way, which would, however, have been more effective without the scarlet which dyed her face.

"A hundred and seventy-five dollars out of the bank! Hoity toity! Well, this *is* business!" said grandpa.

"I suppose I may have my own money to use if I need it," said Del, feeling her color mount higher under grandpa's twinkling eyes.

"Dear me! how old we *are* getting," said grandpa, provokingly. "I feel myself to be the youngest in the family. Soon there'll be no one but Bess who will associate with me."

This joking was more than Del could bear when she was in such trouble.

"I really want the money, grandpa," she said, the tears springing to her eyes.

"Well, well, dear, sit down here, and tell me all about it," said grandpa, making room for her beside him on the piazza seat. To tell all about it was the very last thing that Del intended to do.

"It is quite a private matter, grandpa," she said; "I can't tell any one, and I *must* have the money right away."

"But, my dear child, that money is not to be meddled with, on any account. Your father would be very angry. And a hundred and seventy-five dollars is a great deal of money for a little girl like you. If you have been getting into debt for fol-de-rols—"

"I can't tell you what it is. Oh, grandpa,

please let me have the money, and don't ask me!"

Poor Grandpa Damer had a very soft heart for his grandchildren, and he was finding it very difficult to harden it.

"I shouldn't be doing my duty to you, dear. Doesn't your Aunt Katherine know, or Kate, or anybody? Well, then, I can't, I really can't let you have the money."

This sounded final. In Del's experience grandpa was not coaxable; he yielded at once, or not at all.

She was tempted to tell him all about her trouble, but pride held her back strongly. They had all been inclined to make fun of her friend Jeanne; they had prophesied no good of her grown-up and fashionable airs; it would be very bitter to confess, so soon, that they were right. Besides, they had a horror of borrowing; they would blame her severely, and Del was very sensitive to blame. She *must* manage it without letting any one know.

"I shall have to write to papa; I didn't like to wait, that's all," she said, proudly, turning away, but setting her lips together tightly to keep back a sob.

She went and mounted Jock, and turned his face homeward, and grandpa did not call her back.

But Grandpa Damer, apparently absorbed in his newspaper, was a very miserable man. It cut him to the heart to see Del's bright face clouded, and the temptation to restore its sunshine was almost too great to resist. He tried to think it a trifle, and to forget it in a political leader in which his party was abused, but it was all in vain.

"I am becoming imbecile," he said, as he folded the paper and walked up and down the piazza. "I certainly am. To think of giving that child all that money. Very likely somebody has been imposing upon her. A girl of that age doesn't know chalk from cheese. But she thinks that wisdom would die with her. Their father and mother never ought to have gone away and left me at the mercy of those youngsters, never! I won't go to the Point, not a step!"

And so strong was Grandpa Damer's resolution, that it was not until two hours after breakfast, the next morning, that he found himself in the saddle, and even then he wasn't sure that he should go to Birch Point; he let the reins lie upon old Pegasus's neck, and Pegasus took the responsibility. Perhaps it was a lively recollection of lumps of sugar, dispensed by Kate, which led Pegasus to decide in favor of Birch Point.

Grandpa Damer had just put into his pocketbook two crisp, new, one-hundred dollar bills. He said to himself, somewhat irritably, that he did not know in the least what he should do with them, but it was always well to have money in one's pocket.

Del was not to be seen, and he did not ask for her, but stayed to luncheon, which was contrary to his custom. Del appeared, then, and with so drooping a countenance and such traces of tears that he thought with satisfaction of the two one-hundred-dollar bills, and might not have been able to restrain himself from giving them to her, at once, if he had not left his pocket-book in the pocket of his overcoat, which was hanging in the hall. But he was rather gruff in his manner; that was grandpa's way when he was afraid of being too soft; and Del saw no signs of relenting, and she left the room before luncheon was half over, not feeling sure that she should not break down.

Grandpa Damer wandered about the house, restlessly, after luncheon was over, and then, suddenly, he despatched Bess in search of Del.

Then he went to the pocket of his overcoat which was hanging in the hall. And immediately after there was a great outcry. He called for Aunt Katherine and Diantha and Simeon in a breath.

"I thought a man could hang up his coat

here! I didn't think there was a thief in this house! My pocket-book is gone!" he cried.

All the household came rushing into the hall. Del, coming down the staircase, somewhat slowly and reluctantly, behind Bess, turned very pale.

"Land of Goshen! there hain't been a soul in that hall!" exclaimed Diantha, "unless 'twas —there! I told you, Quintilla, that you hadn't any business to tell Cainy to run out this way, if that pesky cow *was* a-tramplin' down the geraniums! But there, if Cainy is a limb, I never catched him stealin'!"

"He hadn't no time," said Quintilla. "He run as quick as scat. I heard him; he made an awful noise."

"He might have caught a glimpse of the pocket-book, and come back softly," said Aunt Katherine, who had always shared grandpa's doubts of Cainy.

"Oh, grandpa, the lining is ripped away here!" cried Polly, who was investigating.

"You might have lost it before you got here!"

"I might have, but I didn't," said grandpa, grimly. "I felt and saw the pocket-book when I hung the coat up. Go and find Cainy, if he hasn't got too far away by this time. I never expected any good of that boy. I have talked to your father enough about him. I shouldn't have left money there if I had supposed that he ever came into this part of the house. Perhaps it was careless, anyway, but I have done it a great many times."

It was Polly who went in search of Cainy. She found him just returning from a long chase of the trespassing cow. He was whistling along, his hands in his pockets, and his hat on the back of his head, in apparent ease of mind and conscience.

"Cainy, you remember our agreement— you're to tell the truth and I am to believe you," said Polly, impressively. "Have you seen grandpa's pocket-book? It's lost."

Cainy's head drooped; he shuffled uneasily on his feet; apparently as a desperate measure he stood on one foot.

"I hain't *took* it," he said, suddenly lifting his head and looking into Polly's eyes.

"Do you know anything about it. Have you seen it?" asked Polly, wondering at his manner.

Cainy repeated his gymnastic movements.

"Yes, I saw it," he said at length. "I knew 'twas hangin' in his coat-pocket in the hall. But I never took it."

"How did you happen to see it? What do you mean, Cainy?" demanded Polly.

"Well, I was runnin' through the hall and I saw it, because I happened to, I s'pose; that's all," said Cainy.

"Cainy, there was no other boy there, was there? You didn't let any of those dreadful boys in, did you?" said Polly, struck by a new idea.

"No, there wa'n't no boy there, not as I saw," said Cainy, promptly.

Polly began to feel satisfied that Cainy's embarrassment arose merely from the fact that he had seen the pocket-book.

"Come and tell grandpa, then," said Polly.

"He won't b'lieve me," said Cainy, hanging back in evident alarm. "Folks won't never b'lieve me. But I tell you honest, Miss Polly, I don't tell near so many whoppers as I did. They don't seem to come so easy since you 'greed to b'lieve me. But it wouldn't be no use to tell the guv'nor so. He'll have me shet in jail, see if he don't."

"Here's Cainy, grandpa. He didn't take the pocket-book; he says so," said Polly, drawing the extremely reluctant Cainy by his sleeve.

"Humph! he *says* so," said grandpa. "You young rascal, how many lies do you suppose you have told, in your life?"

Cainy looked as if he were considering the matter, but was non-committal.

"I ain't telling 'em no more," he said, at length. "It always did come kind of nat'ral to me, tellin' whoppers did, but I would have tried to quit it before, only it didn't seem no use, because folks wouldn't b'lieve me, nohow. Miss Polly, she 'greed to b'lieve me, and I'm tryin' to quit. I ain't tellin' no whopper, now; sure as you're born, I ain't, sir. I never stole no pocket-book."

"He didn't. Oh, grandpa, don't have him arrested. I'm *sure* he didn't," cried Polly.

"I'll say this for Cainy, me that ain't never denied that he was a limb," said Diantha. "I never did know him to steal."

"I suppose it would be of no use to search him. He has had time enough to hide it a dozen times over," said grandpa;—"if he did take it," he added, a little more kindly. That Polly believed in Cainy impressed grandpa more than he thought wise, or would have wished to acknowledge. "Now, sir, if I don't send for an officer and have you arrested, at once, will you promise Miss Polly that you won't run away?"

"I ain't goin' to run away, nohow. I ain't got nothin' to run away for. I wouldn't tell nobody a whopper about *that*," said Cainy.

"The pocket-book must have gone somewhere," said grandpa. He turned to his coat, and searched it all over. That looked, Polly thought, as if he had some faith in Cainy. Then he looked around the group in a puzzled way, last of all at Del, who sat upon the lowest stair. She looked very pale and worn, and she had tried, once or twice, as if vainly, to open her mouth. Grandpa had seen it, without seeming to look.

"There! there! we'll say no more about it, now," he said. "I'll look further into the matter." And he took his hat and coat and went out.

"I can't believe it! I won't!" he said to himself, as he stood outside. "And yet, how the child looked! To let the boy be suspected, too! No, no! I don't know how I came to think of such a thing. One of the *girls!* I don't see how I could bear it. I've been realizing more and more, lately, how all my earthly comfort and hope is bound up in these children. No, I won't think *that!*"

"Polly! Polly!" Bess followed her, and spoke in a mysterious whisper. "I think I know who took the money, and it wasn't Cainy! Del wanted some money for something; she wanted it orfly. She fell asleep in the hammock, yesterday, and she talked about it in her sleep. And did you see how orfly white she was?"

Polly turned upon her with dilated eyes.

"What *are* you talking about? How can you say such things? Go away, Bess; oh, do go away!"

CHAPTER XIX.

Roy and Lord Brentford were coming back from Moosehead Lake, and Aunt Katherine and Polly went down to the wharf in the carriage to meet them. There had been a heavy fog all day, as heavy as when Polly had taken her memorable voyage in the *High-Flyer*, and the steamer was delayed. She had been due at 5.45 P.M., and it was now nearly 7. Waiting began to seem hopeless. Grandpa, whom they met on the wharf, said that the steamer "couldn't see an inch before her nose," and might have been obliged to put in somewhere for the night, although she seldom did that coming down the river.

Aunt Katherine looked at her watch by the light of the carriage lamp, and said they would wait just ten minutes more; if the steamer had not arrived, then they would go home, and Simeon could return with the carriage. Only ten minutes, and no one thought it would be different from the last ten, except that possibly the steamboat whistle might pierce the fog, and make one believe again that the world beyond the wharf had not slipped off into space. Old Cap'n Lunt, who had been a famous voyager in his day, would go on repeating oft-told tales of wonderful fogs he had seen, careless of the fact that his audience, on the pile of lobster-traps, had dwindled to deaf-and-dumb Jimmy Pearcy from the poor-house, and a socially disposed, wandering puppy; that the group in the shelter of the lobster factory would continue to discuss the strike and the political situation with more or less vigor, and that Tommy French would go on dangling his small legs off the end of the wharf and tooting an ear-splitting horn, with which he seemed to have a vague expectation of hurrying the steamer. Six of the ten minutes had passed, and Tommy French was just raising his horn for a vigorous, impatient toot, when there came a deafening report, like loudest thunder; the wharf trembled on its stanch piles, pieces of timber came flying through the air; some of them struck the carriage, and the horses quivered and snorted with fear, and would have plunged madly off if Simeon had not clung to their heads. In the thick fog and gathering darkness it was impossible to tell what had happened, and there was a wild panic. Amid the cries of "Earthquake" and "Dynamite," Polly heard at length a calmer voice which said something had exploded in Damer's ship-yard, adjoining the wharf; the new counting-room, which had been built on the end of a long, low building, once used as a workshop, but now unoccupied, had been blown up, probably in an effort to blow open the safe, although it was a queer time of night to be trying that.

The buildings, old and new, were in ruins. Was any one killed? Polly listened, breathlessly, for the answer. There was some fear that the governor was in the counting-room; he had been known to be there but a short time before. Polly grew sick and faint. It seemed like a blessed vision when grandpa stepped to the side of the carriage.

"I left the counting-room not five minutes before the explosion," he said. "We shall have to use more desperate measures with these rascals! I only hope they haven't killed anybody. I don't know anything about it. I hurried here to you, knowing you would be frightened."

"We can't tell how many people there may be in the ruins," said some one near by. "There's been one taken out; it's that queer, long-legged fellow who works at Dr. Damer's."

"Cainy! oh, Cainy!" cried Polly.

Her grandfather hurried away, and it was not many minutes before he returned, with some men before him clearing the way, and others carrying a limp and apparently lifeless body.

"Get him into the carriage, quick!" said grandpa. "We can't do less for him, whatever he has done. There is a mob ready to tear him to pieces; they're wild with rage at this last piece of work. Now, Simeon, let the horses go!" he added, as Cainy was placed, as carefully as possible, upon the back seat, and he stepped in, with Simeon, himself. "There are men in front who will clear the way. Is he dead? Oh, no; his arm is broken, I think, and his shoulder crushed, and he has fainted from pain and loss of blood. He probably hasn't got half that he deserves, Polly! He belongs to that gang of desperadoes, and they probably used him to do their dangerous work. If I didn't think the fellow was lacking in brains, I don't suppose I could feel like showing him any mercy. He never ought to have been kept in the house.

I've talked to your father enough about him!"

Polly felt bewildered; even when they had got beyond the jarring crowd she could scarcely think. Grandpa's words seemed to her hard; she could not believe Cainy had been as guilty as he thought. A new possibility, of which she dared not speak, had struck her with benumbing force—where was Syd?

A few minutes later Cainy had come to himself, on a settee in the hall where he had been laid pending the arrival of the surgeon who had been sent for.

"You just let me go!" he said, eagerly, trying to rise. "I sha'n't know what they're goin' to do, and then I can't stop 'em! But what was it that happened? I was trying to hide away in that closet, in the old workshop, so'st' I could overhear 'em, and find out whether they meant to burn the new ship that's on the stocks, or this house. I'm master afraid it's this house!" Cainy started up again, but dropped back from weakness. "What was it that happened? I was getting into that closet, and what an all-fired bang that was! And it seemed as if the world flew all to pieces."

"Tell us all about it, as plainly as you can, my boy, but don't try to talk if it hurts you," said grandpa, kindly.

"They was goin' to have a meetin' in the old workshop to-night, the Red Revs was," said Cainy, speaking faintly but very distinctly. "They've been havin' 'em there ever since—ever since they couldn't have 'em in another place. They made Syd get 'em the key. They've been plannin' to do something orfle, and I thought if I could find out jest what it was I could stop 'em. I don't know as I should have thought of doin' it, once; I've felt kind of different, every way, sence Miss Polly 'greed to b'lieve me. And she said her father ' had great hopes of me!' They'd kill me if they caught me, I was sure. They don't care whether I go to their meet'n's or not; they don't think I'm so smart as some, and mebbe I ain't. There's been times when I thought so myself, and then again I wa'n't sure. But they'd do most anything to me if they caught me tellin.' There's two fellers that has to go to the meet'n's if they do feel orfle about it now; they've threatened to kill 'em if they don't. And they b'long. If the Red Revs get found out, why they're found out too; and they can't stand that. Did the old workshop fly all to pieces? They can't have no meet'n' there to-night, can they?"

"I don't think they'll have a meeting to-night," said grandpa. "Haven't you any idea what it was that caused the explosion? Was anybody in the counting-room?"

He had listened to Cainy with a perplexed face, but Polly could see that he believed him.

"No, there wa'n't a livin' soul in the countin'-room, nor anywheres round," said Cainy. "I see you go away before I dared to try to get in. I broke a winder in the workshop, and I had a candle and some matches. I don't know what it could have been that blowed up. Seemed as if 'twas right in that closet, 'mongst some boxes and bottles of stuff that Syd and Bruce Bennett put in there; they had 'em up here in the old wing, and then, all of a sudden, they carried 'em down there. Mebbe I hadn't ought to tell," added Cainy, in sudden alarm; "they was ortle private about 'em; they had the closet door all nailed up. I drawed the nails out with a hammer, and then I kind of stuck 'em into the holes again, so'st' they couldn't find out, without tryin' the door, that it had been opened."

"*Syd! Syd!*" repeated grandpa, in tones of wonder and dismay.

"It hadn't nothin' to do with the Revs, sir," said Cainy, eagerly. "Anyhow, I don't think it had, for I heard Syd say they wasn't to know there was anything in the closet."

"You must give me the names of this gang,

every one of them, and tell me everything that you know about them," said grandpa, firmly, but he looked as if he dreaded what he might hear, and Polly knew that he was thinking of Syd.

"I'm willin' to, sir. I knew that was what I'd got to do if I found out what they was goin' to do. I b'long. Cainy Green is one of the names, and it's my princerples that everybody had ought to be rich, as they say, but it can't make nobody rich to destroy folkses property, as I see; and when it's folks that's been good to me, and never kep' back the preserves, and had hopes of me, I couldn't stand no more of it."

"Oh, what is the matter with Cainy? He isn't killed?"

Del had come flying down-stairs, and caught sight of Cainy's white face and the bloodstains upon his clothes.

"Oh, Cainy, you were so good not to tell of me, and I was so mean to let them suspect you! I took the pocket-book! Oh, wait, listen; don't look at me like that, grandpa! I wanted the money so dreadfully, and, although I had written to papa, it would take so long to get an answer. I had to send *poste-restante*, you know, and they were probably travelling; and I saw the pocket-book and I thought it would be so easy to tell you about it, and pay it back when the money came. And Cainy saw me with it in my hand. I only carried it to the head of the stairs. It came over me, all at once, that I had done a dreadful thing, and I ran back and slipped it into the pocket."

Grandpa drew a long breath of relief, and put his arm around her.

"But what became of it, then?" he said, wrinkling his brows.

"I was in a hurry, and I must have slipped it in between the torn lining and the outside. It went down behind the hat-rack; why didn't we think to look there? When Quintilla moved the rack to sweep to-day she found it. I went out to The Bend as fast as I could go; they didn't know where you were, but I told Aaron to tell you the pocket-book was found."

"I had brought the money to give to you, Del," said grandpa. "I am not sure that it is wise to give so much to a little girl who will not tell what she is going to do with it, but since you are so distressed about it—"

"I am not distressed about it now, grandpa; only because I took the pocket-book and let Cainy be suspected. I couldn't think what could have become of it, but I was sure he hadn't taken it because it was only a minute before you came out from lunch that I put it back, and Cainy was driving the cow down the road. It was *good* of you, Cainy! I can't think what made you so good!" said Del, frankly.

"Folks wouldn't have b'lieved what I said, anyhow," said Cainy, "nobody but Miss Polly;

and she'd have felt a sight worse to think it was you than to think it was me; and when folks has been good to me, and b'lieved me, and said they had hopes of me, I ain't goin' to fetch trouble on 'em."

When grandpa came down-stairs, after seeing the surgeon set Cainy's arm and make him as comfortable as possible, he said, and his voice was really a trifle unsteady,

"Well, well, Polly, your father and you were right about that boy after all! There's some good stuff in him. Where there's gratitude there's hope. We shall make a man of him yet!" And then his face clouded suddenly. "I want to see Syd! Does anybody know where Syd is?" he said.

"He went away directly after breakfast, and he hasn't been home since," said Aunt Katherine. "He often goes fishing on these foggy days," she added, but she looked troubled.

"I want to tell you why I don't need the

money now, grandpa," said Del. "Something has turned out so very queerly. But I suppose you are too anxious about the explosion to hear it now."

"Yes, another time, dear; another time. I'm glad it turned out so *well*. I must go, now, and find out the extent of the damage. It's a grave matter, and I'm anxious, I'm very anxious about Syd."

"After all, I don't think I shall ever tell any one all about it," said Del to herself, in the privacy of her own room, after her grandfather had gone. "There is no need of it; they know the worst of me, and much worse it is than I ever knew of myself before. I shall always be afraid of myself after this; queer of Aunt Katherine to say it was a good sign to be afraid of one's self! They'll only laugh about the earrings, if I tell them. That is a perfectly cruel letter of Aunt Augusta's, but, oh, what a relief it was!"

Del drew the letter from her desk to read,

"*Del drew the letter from her desk to read for about the tenth time.*"

for about the tenth time. And this is what she read:

"My dear Niece,—What you wrote me about the earring is no more than I thought likely enough to happen. You needn't suffer any more distress of mind about it, though I'm thinking a little of that won't hurt you, and there's more learned that way than any other. As I say, you needn't suffer any more about it, and you needn't pay for it, or buy one like it, for I have a great assortment of the same kind! I keep them for the benefit of people who want to steal or borrow; going about, as I do, one meets many of those people. I find those little paste imitations, that come very cheap, a great protection to my diamonds, and you see, yourself, how useful they are to protect the feelings of people who happen to lose one! How could you think, my dear, that I'd lend my diamonds to chits like you and Flibbertigibbet? Well, you've got your lesson, and if you got it hard so much the longer will it last you! As for Flibbertigibbet, you can tell her the same thing that I told her the day we met, it's a fine thing to know paste from diamonds!—Your affectionate aunt, Augusta Damer."

"I think it was dreadful of her to deceive me so," said Del to herself; "but, oh, how thankful I am that they were only paste! I think I will tell Polly; she can keep a—"

"Oh, Del!" Bess put her head in at the door, breathless with eagerness, "Syd has run away!"

CHAPTER XX.

"YES, he *has* run away!" persisted Bess, in answer to Del's incredulous look. "Roy and the English boy have come, and they say so. When the steamboat stopped at Belrock, they saw Syd and Bruce Bennett getting out of a rowboat; it was the *Licketty-Split*, Bruce Bennett's boat. Roy said he happened to see the name through the fog; he was sure no other boat ever had that name, so he looked to see who the boys were. Syd had a bag, and Bruce had a bundle. Grandpa thinks they meant to take the cars at Belrock. He has telegraphed everywhere, but he can't tell which way they have gone, and they may get away down to St. John or away on to New York before they are stopped. They put the stuff in that blew up, that's why they're gone."

"Those boys!" exclaimed Del. She had always been absorbed in her own affairs, and she had a settled conviction that boys were a nuisance; but Syd was her brother, and Del felt this new trouble to be so great that what she had just gone through seemed but a trifle in comparison. "I wish I had thought more about Syd. I might have looked after him a little. Oh, I have been so selfish and silly!" she said, rather to herself than to Bess.

"You'd think Polly would be wild, she was always so fond of Syd," said Bess. "But she's just as still as can be, only orfly pale, and can't say her r's at all. And she says she doesn't believe Syd did it, or meant to, or there's some mistake. Just think how foolish, when Cainy knows they put the stuff in the closet, and Syd has run away and all. Oh, and Roy is dividing his snakes with the English boy. He is going away in the morning."

"The English boy" went away the next

morning. He spoke very sympathetically to Polly about Syd just before he left.

"You mustn't believe that Syd did what they say," said Polly, earnestly. "I am sure he didn't, because he promised me that he wouldn't do dreadful things. Whatever they may say, I know that he didn't do it."

"I shall tell him that when I meet him in New York," said Lord Brentford. Polly smiled at that, sad as she was; they had very often smiled at the English boy's idea of space in America. He had not yet been in New York, and seemed, so Polly thought, to believe that he should be likely to see every one who was there, as one might in a little country village. But afterwards Polly found out what he meant.

Telegrams had been sent in every direction, and detectives despatched in search of the runaways, and grandpa held himself in readiness to follow the first clew that appeared. Now and then a false one drew him a short distance only to come back baffled. The boys had left their rowboat at the landing at Belrock, and it seemed that no one had observed them afterwards. The crowd and commotion consequent upon the steamer's arrival had drawn attention away from them, and the heavy fog had further favored their escape. It might have swallowed them up utterly, for anything that appeared to the contrary. It was a time of terrible anxiety and suspense. Polly grew thin and white, and chafed miserably over the fact that she was a girl and could not go in search of Syd. She even made desperate plans to go, in the long, wakeful nights, which were always nullified by common-sense, which came back, as it is apt to do, with daylight.

The Red Revs, as Cainy called them, were all arrested, and the leaders, Nick Hiffley and three other youths of eighteen and nineteen, received their just deserts in the shape of long terms of imprisonment, while the younger boys, who were proven to have followed the leaders generally under the pressure of threats, were released, upon promise of future good behavior. And Cainy, who was slowly recovering from his injuries, declared that he was "gladder to be quit of b'longin' to them Red Revs than he would be to be 'lected president."

Not long after the league came to an end the strikes were peacefully settled; but this consummation, which he had so desired, seemed to bring no comfort now to Grandpa Damer. When not away following some clew, he sat in his office waiting for telegrams and letters. And, after all, it was Polly to whom the first news came—a telegram signed with Lord Brentford's name: "Have found S., safe and innocent. You will receive letter to-morrow."

"Safe and innocent! *innocent*, just as I said!" cried Polly, as grandpa, who had been sent for, came in before they had ceased to laugh and cry over the telegram. Grandpa shook his head doubtfully, although his face had brightened, and he looked to Polly very much as if he would have liked to laugh and cry himself. " Why doesn't he come home then? I don't understand it. Lord Brentford should have telegraphed where he was to be found."

"Only have a little patience, grandpa, and be sure everything is right!" cried Polly. "And isn't he the *nicest* boy?—that was what he meant by saying ' if he should meet Syd in New York;' he has been hunting for him!"

"I don't understand how he could find him when the detectives couldn't. It's all very mysterious," said grandpa.

As we all know, in spite of the almanac, there is the very greatest difference in the length of days. Polly has been heard to say that if she should live to be as old as Methuselah she should never expect to see another twenty-four hours drag themselves along so interminably as those which elapsed between the reception of the English boy's telegram and his letter.

But as all things come at last to him who knows how to wait, so some things come to those who do not, and the letter was promptly delivered into Polly's own hands at the post-office next day. And it was read by her to a family party in the carriage, including Cainy on the driver's seat, letting the horse go at his own sweet will.

"Dear Miss Polly,—I will be as brief and explicit as possible, knowing how anxious you all must be. Your brother and his friend ran away, not because they were guilty of any dynamite deeds or projects, but because of the increasing wickedness of that gang of young ruffians in which they were to be compelled to share, and which they unfortunately had not the courage to divulge. When one considers the age and desperate character of some of those fellows, it is not to be wondered at that they were intimidated."

"That's kind of him to make a little excuse for Syd," interpolated Polly.

"I am not at all sure that he deserves it," said grandpa, grimly. "However, go on, Polly, go on!"

"There is no doubt that they joined the gang with a vague idea of doing something daring and exciting, but with no comprehension of its real purposes. They had not been obliged to take any part in the outrages perpetrated by the older members of the gang, but the latter had evidently concluded that it would be safer to make them sharers in their guilt. They were to have been forced to assist in setting fire to the ship-yards, which was the cause of their running away. It was just as the extreme coldness of the world to empty-pocketed and friendless boys had induced them to think of returning that they read an account of the explosion in the papers, and decided that a cold world with freedom was more desirable than a prison. For they *were* responsible for the explosives. They had hidden in the closet of the workshop a quantity of chemicals which they had used in attempting to get up some stereopticon pictures; they had pursued this art, not very successfully, I judge, for some time, in great privacy in the old wing; and these chemicals had once exploded, the boys tell me, with a noise as loud as a pistol-shot, but without doing any particular damage."

"I heard it!" cried Polly. "That was early in the summer before Lord Brentford came! And that was the queer bubbling noise!"

"Go on! Polly, go on!" cried a chorus.

"A more dangerous industry which they have practised in the same place was the making of Chinese fireworks. Bruce Bennett, it seems, had an uncle who has lived in China, and who was so injudicious as to instruct him in the art. They did not succeed in making a supply for the Fourth of July, as they hoped to, but practised at intervals, hoping to be ready for next year's celebration. When his privacy was invaded, Syd says, they carried their materials to the workshop for safe-keeping. The Red Revs, he says, forced him to allow them to have meetings in the old wing, but they became frightened and came but twice. They say they were somewhat afraid to move the explosives, but thought they were safe in the closet. Syd thinks a spark from Cainy's candle must have come in contact with the powder. They were, you see, guilty of nothing but extreme carelessness, which, however blameworthy, is quite different to a criminal intention."

"Of *course, quite* different!" exclaimed Polly, exultantly. "Oh, poor Syd!"

"The young knaves! It's a wonder you were not all burned in your beds," said grandpa. But it was easy to read the happy relief in his look.

"I came upon the boys almost by accident, at last, and after I had almost despaired of finding them. And then it was under such circumstances that they could and would have slipped away from me if I had not promised not to betray them. They have been reduced to sore straits, and have suffered greatly. I found them about to join a show of the lowest character; they were to help take care of the animals in payment for their passage to the far West, Bruce Bennett cherishing a somewhat subdued and flickering ambition to become a cowboy. The terms of the contract did not include board, and they had no money and were extremely hungry, yet Bruce Bennett absolutely refuses to return, and Syd was only induced to by the knowledge that *you* had always believed him innocent.

"'Old Polly has stood up for me, has she?' he said, and for the first time he quite broke down, and his hard and hopeless mood vanished. I must tell you, Miss Polly, that a little text of the New Testament came into my mind: 'Thou hast gained thy brother.' And

I must also take the liberty to tell you that although I misunderstood you, at first—I think a fellow is likely to, American girls are so different to English ones, you know—after I knew you better you kept me from being homesick, because you were so simple and natural, and not affected or young-ladyish, so that I was afraid of you. You seemed so like my own sisters."

"Oh, oh! if that isn't the greatest!" cried Del. "And I always thought he was more horror-stricken at Polly than at any of us."

"There, I don't care about that flummery; read when Syd is coming home!" said grandpa.

"As soon as some necessary changes in his appearance are effected, Syd will leave for home. I wish I could go with him, but I think he prefers to go alone, as it shows that he goes voluntarily. Bruce Bennett persists in following the show, but has promised me that he will write to his father as soon as he reaches Chicago, and I am quite sure that by that time he will be quite willing to return."

"You mustn't say a hard word to Syd, not one; must you, grandpa? he has suffered so much," said Polly, eagerly.

"You seem to be mistress of this situation, Captain Polly," said grandpa, good-naturedly; "and I've no doubt I shall kill the fatted calf to please you. But the young rascal deserved to suffer!"

But Polly need not have feared. When Syd arrived his looks were a sufficient plea for pardon. They would have softened a far harder heart than Grandpa Damer's.

Thin and haggard and dejected, with all his jaunty independence gone, Polly could scarcely have believed that it was Syd if he had not called her "Old Polly" (Syd's strongest term of endearment) in one breath, and told her "not to act like a girl, and make a great fuss," in the next. It was very evident that *he* was struggling with a very large lump in his throat, and in danger of making a great fuss himself; and oh, how pitifully glad he was to get home, and what an appetite he had, after a while, for the goodies of which Diantha had cooked enough for an army, knowing, as she declared, that "one of the things there wa'n't no reck'nin' on was a hungry boy."

He was Syd still, no doubt, with all his "trying" ways, his discouraging lack of candor, and his susceptibility to bad influences; but he had had a lesson, and he could learn. A boy is never a hopeless case who can learn. And Polly was brimming over with faith and joy. She had one great excuse always ready for Syd. "I ought to have told about that dreadful society, even if I *had* promised," she would say. "That might have prevented all the trouble."

Strangely enough, Syd and his grandfather had changed places in their opinions about Syd's going away to school. Syd was now

"And oh, what an appetite he had!"

anxious to go, and his grandfather wished him to stay at home and "live down" his disgrace, especially as he had been assured by Bruce Bennett's father that Bruce would go away to school.

It was only a few days after Syd's return that Cainy, almost recovered from his injuries and in the best of spirits, although he still wore his arm in a sling, came, somewhat shamefacedly, to Polly, and remarked:

"Me and some of the fellers was thinkin' of makin' you a little present." (Polly understood at once that the fellers were "patch" boys.) "Joe Banks says that the old *High-Flyer* has come ashore, down by Pemetic light; Joe's brother he keeps the light; and the young ones have took her for a playhouse, jest as you used to have her. She's consid'able stove up, but me 'n the fellers calc'lated that we could tow her up if you'd like to have her. But I told 'em I'd ask you first, for, says I, it would be jest like my Miss Polly not to want her took away from them young ones, and—"

"Oh, no, Cainy, I shouldn't. It was very kind and thoughtful of you and the other boys, but that is just what I should have wished to happen to the old boat. I wonder if there was any candy left in her, and what did they think of her? Some day we must take a sail down there and find out."

Grandpa Damer said, that little English lord was a capital fellow, *capital*, and he was going to invite him to come down to the great harvest-home and barn-warming which he was going to have when the new barn was done.

Del prophesied that he wouldn't come; she said he had put them all into his note-book, and labelled them—he always labelled his snakes and bugs—"Queer young Yankees discovered in remote regions," and then forgotten all about them. Grandpa said he *might* have labelled them "The sorrows of a poor old man," but he thought that, after all, he had liked them well enough to come again.

And he did come, and Harry was at home with a party of friends, and I only wish I had space to tell you what a great time it was! Grandpa *would* invite everybody, and even Del didn't object, but said that if Jeanne Higgins *had* kept her promise to have her invited to Lenox she should have stayed at home on this account.

The bare inside of the great barn was hidden under green foliage and blossoms, and gay Chinese lanterns swung everywhere. There was an orchestra from Portland, but grandpa declared that "Aaron's nose should not be put out of joint," and he played 'Come lasses and lads' to his own and grandpa's hearts' content. Cainy, in a brand-new suit, with a button-hole bouquet, acted as usher, and showed so much discretion in this difficult capacity as to make many people say he "had plenty of sense after all." I, for one, have never doubted it. Roy seemed to have left his wrinkle quite behind him, and Syd, with a subdued and more responsible look, was winning his old place in every one's regard—perhaps more than his old place, for every one recognizes the nobility of living down disgrace and making our faults "stepping-stones to higher things."

And Polly, dear red-headed, tender-hearted Polly, as she footed it gayly through the dance, heard a sweeter sound than the music of the violins; a still small voice that whispered, over and over, to her heart, "Thou hast gained thy brother."

THE END.

INTERESTING BOOKS FOR YOUNG PEOPLE.

Published by HARPER & BROTHERS.

☞ HARPER & BROTHERS *will send their publications by mail, postage prepaid, to any part of the United States, Canada, or Mexico, on receipt of the price.*

THE WONDER CLOCK; or, Four-and-Twenty Marvellous Tales: Being One for each Hour of the Day. Written and Illustrated with 160 Drawings by HOWARD PYLE. Embellished with Verses by KATHARINE PYLE. Large 8vo, Ornamental Cloth, $3 00.

PEPPER AND SALT; or, Seasoning for Young Folks. Prepared and Profusely Illustrated by HOWARD PYLE. 4to, Illuminated Cloth, $2 00.

THOMAS W. KNOX'S WORKS. 8vo, Cloth. Profusely Illustrated.
    THE BOY TRAVELLERS IN MEXICO. $3 00.
    THE BOY TRAVELLERS IN AUSTRALASIA. $3 00.
    THE BOY TRAVELLERS ON THE CONGO. Adventures of Two Youths in a Journey with Henry M. Stanley "Through the Dark Continent." $3 00.
    THE BOY TRAVELLERS IN THE RUSSIAN EMPIRE. $3 00.
    THE BOY TRAVELLERS IN SOUTH AMERICA. A Journey through Ecuador, Peru, Bolivia, Brazil, Paraguay, Argentine Republic, and Chili. With Descriptions of Voyages upon the Amazon and La Plata Rivers. $3 00.
    THE VOYAGE OF THE "VIVIAN," to the North Pole and Beyond. Adventures of Two Youths in the Open Polar Sea. $2 50.
    THE BOY TRAVELLERS IN THE FAR EAST. Five Parts. $3 00 each. The Five Parts in a Box, $15 00.
        PART I. JAPAN AND CHINA.
        PART II. SIAM AND JAVA. With Descriptions of Cochin China, Cambodia, Sumatra, and the Malay Archipelago.
        PART III. CEYLON AND INDIA. With Descriptions of Borneo, the Philippine Islands, and Burmah.
        PART IV. EGYPT AND THE HOLY LAND.
        PART V. JOURNEY THROUGH AFRICA.
    HUNTING ADVENTURES ON LAND AND SEA. Two Parts. $2 50 each.
        PART I. THE YOUNG NIMRODS IN NORTH AMERICA.
        PART II. THE YOUNG NIMRODS AROUND THE WORLD.

CHARLES CARLETON COFFIN'S WORKS. Seven Volumes. Copiously Illustrated. Square 8vo, Cloth, $3 00 each.
    THE STORY OF LIBERTY.   THE BOYS OF '76.
    OLD TIMES IN THE COLONIES.   BUILDING THE NATION.
    DRUM-BEAT OF THE NATION.   MARCHING TO VICTORY.
        REDEEMING THE REPUBLIC.

Interesting Books for Young People.

INDIAN HISTORY FOR YOUNG FOLKS. By Francis S. Drake. Copiously Illustrated. 8vo, Cloth, $3 00.

HARPER'S YOUNG PEOPLE. Volumes IX. (1888) and VIII. (1887), 4to, Cloth, $3 50 each. (Volumes I., II., III., IV., V., VI., and VII., *out of print*.) Each Volume contains the Numbers for a year, with over 800 pages and about 700 Illustrations.

HARPER'S YOUNG PEOPLE SERIES. Ill'd. 16mo, Cloth, $1 00 per vol.

Toby Tyler; or, Ten Weeks with a Circus.—Mr. Stubbs's Brother (Sequel to "Toby Tyler").—Tim and Tip.—Raising the "Pearl."—Left Behind; or, Ten Days a Newsboy.—Silent Pete. By James Otis.

The Moral Pirates.—The Cruise of the "Ghost."—The Cruise of the Canoe Club.—The Adventures of Jimmy Brown.—A New Robinson Crusoe. By W. L. Alden.

Mildred's Bargain, and Other Stories.—Nan.—Rolf House.—Jo's Opportunity.—The Story of Music and Musicians.—The Colonel's Money.—The Household of Glen Holly. By Lucy C. Lillie.

Who was Paul Grayson? By John Habberton.

The Four Macnicols. By William Black.

The Talking Leaves: An Indian Story.—Two Arrows. A Story of Red and White. By W. O. Stoddard.

The Ice Queen. By Ernest Ingersoll.

The Lost City; or, The Boy Explorers in Central Asia.—Into Unknown Seas. By David Ker.

Prince Lazybones, and Other Stories. By Mrs. J. W. Hays.

Strange Stories from History for Young People. By G. Cary Eggleston.

Wakulla: A Story of Adventure in Florida.—The Flamingo Feather.—Derrick Sterling.—Crystal, Jack & Co. and Delta Bixby. By C. K. Munroe.

Uncle Peter's Trust. By Geo. B. Perry.

DIDDIE, DUMPS, AND TOT; OR, PLANTATION CHILD-LIFE. By Louise Clarke-Pyrnelle. Illustrated. 16mo, Cloth, $1 00.

NEW GAMES FOR PARLOR AND LAWN. By G. B. Bartlett. 16mo, Cloth, $1 00.

FROM THE FORECASTLE TO THE CABIN. By Capt. S. Samuels. Illustrated. 12mo, Extra Cloth, $1 50.

POLITICS FOR YOUNG AMERICANS. By Charles Nordhoff. 12mo, Half Leather, 75 cents; Paper, 40 cents.

GOD AND THE FUTURE LIFE. The Reasonableness of Christianity. By Charles Nordhoff. 16mo, Cloth, $1 00.

ANIMAL LIFE IN THE SEA AND ON THE LAND. A Zoology for Young People. By Sarah Cooper. Profusely Ill'd. 12mo, Cloth, $1 25.

THE BALL OF THE VEGETABLES, and Other Stories in Prose and Verse. By Margaret Eytinge. Illustrated. 8vo, Cloth, $2 00.

THE HISTORY OF A MOUNTAIN. By Élisée Reclus. Illustrated by L. Bennett. 12mo, Cloth, $1 25.

THE ADVENTURES OF A YOUNG NATURALIST. By Lucien Biart. With 117 Illustrations. 12mo, Cloth, $1 75.

AN INVOLUNTARY VOYAGE. By Lucien Biart. Illustrated. 12mo, Cloth, $1 25.

THE BOYHOOD OF MARTIN LUTHER. By Henry Mayhew. Illustrated. 16mo, Cloth, $1 25.

THE STORY OF THE PEASANT-BOY PHILOSOPHER. (Founded on the Early Life of Ferguson, the Shepherd-Boy Astronomer.) By Henry Mayhew. 16mo, Cloth, $1 25.

YOUNG BENJAMIN FRANKLIN. By Henry Mayhew. Illustrated. 16mo, Cloth, $1 25.

THE WONDERS OF SCIENCE; or, Young Humphry Davy. The Life of a Wonderful Boy. By Henry Mayhew. 16mo, Cloth, $1 25.

THE BOYHOOD OF GREAT MEN. By John G. Edgar. Illustrated. 16mo, Cloth, $1 00.

THE FOOTPRINTS OF FAMOUS MEN. By John G. Edgar. Illustrated. 16mo, Cloth, $1 00.

HISTORY FOR BOYS; or, Annals of the Nations of Modern Europe. By John G. Edgar. Illustrated. 16mo, Cloth, $1 00.

SEA-KINGS AND NAVAL HEROES. A Book for Boys. By John G. Edgar. Illustrated. 16mo, Cloth, $1 00.

THE WARS OF THE ROSES. By John G. Edgar. Illustrated. 16mo, Cloth, $1 00.

Interesting Books for Young People.

HOW TO GET STRONG, AND HOW TO STAY SO. By WILLIAM BLAIKIE. With Illustrations. 16mo, Cloth, $1 00; Paper, 50 cents.

SOUND BODIES FOR OUR BOYS AND GIRLS. By WILLIAM BLAIKIE. Illustrated. 16mo, Cloth, 40 cents.

DOGS AND THEIR DOINGS. By Rev. F. O. MORRIS, B.A. Illustrated. Square 8vo, Cloth, Gilt Sides, $1 75.

TALES FROM THE ODYSSEY FOR BOYS AND GIRLS. By C. M. B. 32mo, Paper, 25 cents; Cloth, 40 cents.

CAST UP BY THE SEA; or, The Adventures of Ned Gray. By Sir SAMUEL W. BAKER. Illustrated. 12mo, Cloth, $1 25; 4to, Paper, 15 cents.

THE ADVENTURES OF REUBEN DAVIDGER; Seventeen Years and Four Months Captive among the Dyaks of Borneo. By J. GREENWOOD. 8vo, Cloth, $1 25; 4to, Paper, 15 cents.

WILD SPORTS OF THE WORLD. A Book of Natural History and Adventure. By JAMES GREENWOOD. Illustrated. Crown 8vo, Cloth, $2 50.

HOMES WITHOUT HANDS: Being a Description of the Habitations of Animals. By the Rev. J. G. WOOD, M.A., F.L.S. With about 140 Illustrations. 8vo, Cloth, $4 50; Sheep, $5 00; Half Calf, $6 75.

THE ILLUSTRATED NATURAL HISTORY. By the Rev. J. G. WOOD. M.A., F.L.S. With 450 Engravings. 12mo, Cloth, $1 05.

CAMP LIFE IN THE WOODS; and the Tricks of Trapping and Trap Making. By W. HAMILTON GIBSON, Author of "Pastoral Days." Illustrated. 12mo, Cloth, $1 00.

NIMROD OF THE SEA; or, The American Whaleman. By WILLIAM M. DAVIS. With many Illustrations. 12mo, Cloth, $2 00.

ODD PEOPLE: Being a Popular Description of Singular Races of Man. By Captain MAYNE REID. With Illustrations. 16mo, Cloth, 75 cents.

COUNTRY COUSINS. Short Studies in the Natural History of the United States. By ERNEST INGERSOLL. Illustrated. 8vo, Cloth, $2 50.

FRIENDS WORTH KNOWING. Glimpses of American Natural History. By ERNEST INGERSOLL. Illustrated. 16mo, Cloth, $1 00.

PAUL B. DU CHAILLU'S WORKS ON AFRICA. Five Volumes. Illustrated. 12mo, Cloth, $1 50 each.
    THE COUNTRY OF THE DWARFS.   MY APINGI KINGDOM.
    WILD LIFE UNDER THE EQUATOR.   LOST IN THE JUNGLE.
    STORIES OF THE GORILLA COUNTRY.

ROUND THE WORLD; including a Residence in Victoria, and a Journey by Rail across North America. By a Boy. Edited by SAMUEL SMILES. Illustrated. 12mo, Cloth, $1 50.

THE SELF-HELP SERIES. By S. SMILES. 12mo, Cloth, $1 00 each.
    SELF-HELP.   CHARACTER.   THRIFT.   DUTY.

STORIES OF INVENTORS AND DISCOVERERS in Science and the Useful Arts. By JOHN TIMBS. Illustrated. 12mo, Cloth, $1 50.

OUR CHILDREN'S SONGS. Illustrated. 8vo, Cloth, $1 00.

FAMOUS LONDON MERCHANTS. A Book for Boys. By H. R. Fox BOURNE. Illustrated. 16mo, Cloth, $1 00.

PRAIRIE AND FOREST. A Description of the Game of North America, with Personal Adventures in their Pursuit. By PARKER GILLMORE. Illustrated. 12mo, Cloth, $1 50.

PUSS-CAT MEW, and Other New Fairy Stories for my Children. By E. H. KNATCHBULL-HUGESSEN. Illustrated. 12mo, Cloth, $1 25.

FAIRY TALES OF ALL NATIONS. By ÉDOUARD LABOULAYE. Translated by MARY L. BOOTH. Illustrated. 12mo, Cloth, Bevelled Edges, $2 00; Gilt Edges, $2 50.

LAST FAIRY TALES. By ÉDOUARD LABOULAYE. Translated by MARY L. BOOTH. Illustrated. 12mo, Cloth, Bevelled Edges, $2 00; Gilt Edges, $2 50.

Interesting Books for Young People.

THE THOUSAND AND ONE NIGHTS; or, The Arabian Nights' Entertainments. Translated and Arranged for Family Reading by E. W. LANE. 600 Illustrations. 2 vols., 12mo, Cloth, $3 50.

JACOB ABBOTT'S WORKS.

SCIENCE FOR THE YOUNG. Illustrated. 4 vols., 12mo, Cloth, $1 50 each.
- HEAT.
- LIGHT.
- WATER AND LAND.
- FORCE.

FRANCONIA STORIES. Illustrated. 16mo, Cloth, 75 cents each.
- MALLEVILLE.
- MARY BELL.
- ELLEN LINN.
- WALLACE.
- BEECHNUT.
- STUYVESANT.
- AGNES.
- MARY ERSKINE.
- RODOLPHUS.
- CAROLINE.

LITTLE LEARNER SERIES. Illustrated. 16mo, Cloth, 75 cents each.
- LEARNING TO TALK.
- LEARNING TO THINK.
- LEARNING ABOUT COMMON THINGS.
- LEARNING ABOUT RIGHT AND WRONG.
- LEARNING TO READ.

MARCO PAUL SERIES. Marco Paul's Voyages and Travels in the Pursuit of Knowledge. Illustrated. 16mo, Cloth, 75 cents each.
- IN NEW YORK.
- ON THE ERIE CANAL.
- IN THE FORESTS OF MAINE.
- IN VERMONT.
- IN BOSTON.
- AT THE SPRINGFIELD ARMORY.

RAINBOW AND LUCKY SERIES. Illustrated. 16mo, Cloth, 75 cents each.
- HANDIE.
- RAINBOW'S JOURNEY.
- UP THE RIVER.
- THE THREE PINES.
- SELLING LUCKY.

YOUNG CHRISTIAN SERIES. Illustrated. 12mo, Cloth, $1 75 each.
- THE YOUNG CHRISTIAN.
- THE CORNER STONE.
- THE WAY TO DO GOOD.
- HOARYHEAD AND M'DONNER.

THE YOUNG CHRISTIAN. A Memorial Volume. With a Sketch of the Author by one of his Sons. Steel Plate Portrait of the Author, and Wood cuts. 12mo, Cloth, $2 00.

www.ingramcontent.com/pod-product-compliance
Lightning Source LLC
Chambersburg PA
CBHW031857220426
43663CB00006B/668